# DK

## LONDON, NEW YORK,
## MELBOURNE, MUNICH, AND DELHI

**Senior editor** Niki Foreman
**Senior art editor** Philip Letsu

**Project editors** Fran Jones, Ashwin Khurana
**Designers** Mik Gates, Katie Knutton,
Hoa Luc, Jacqui Swan

**Editors** Jenny Finch, Andrea Mills
**Additional design** Daniela Boraschi, Spencer Holbrook

**Managing editor** Linda Esposito
**Managing art editors** Jim Green, Diane Thistlethwaite
**Category publisher** Laura Buller

**Jacket designer** Yumiko Tahata
**Jacket editor** Matilda Gollon
**Design development manager** Sophia M. Tampakopoulos Turner

**Creative retouching** Steve Willis
**Picture research** Jenny Faithfull

**DK picture librarian** Lucy Claxton
**Production editor** Clare McLean
**Senior production controller** Angela Graef

First published in the United States in 2010 by
DK Publishing, 375 Hudson Street,
New York, New York 10014

DK books are available at special discounts when purchased in bulk for
sales promotions, premiums, fundraising, or educational use. For details, contact:
DK Publishing Special Markets
375 Hudson Street
New York, New York 10014
SpecialSales@dk.com

A catalog record for this book is
available from the Library of Congress.

ISBN: 978-0-7566-6739-9

Color reproduction by MDP, United Kingdom
Printed and bound by Toppan, China

**Discover more at
www.dk.com**

# DANGER!

**Written by:**

Laura Buller, Susan Kennedy, Jim Pipe, Richard Walker

**Consultants:**

Kim Bryan, Lisa Burke, David Hughes, Philip Parker

# CONTENTS

# NATURE'S NASTIES

Nature may look lovely, but it's also full of unpleasant surprises… so watch your back and stay on your toes as nature reveals its sinister side. From pretty plants with sneaky secrets to cuddly creatures that kill, nature sure can have a nasty sting in its tail. Proceed with caution!

# WANTED

## THE WILD BUNCH

### HARRY "THE HISSER" SNAKE

#### WATCH YOUR STEP!

ALMOST 90,000 FATALITIES A YEAR FROM DEADLY SNAKEBITES

HIS HISSING MIGHT GIVE THE GAME AWAY, BUT THIS SLIPPERY CUSTOMER IS ADEPT AT HIDING AND MIGHT CATCH YOU UNAWARES. NOT ALL SNAKES ARE DANGEROUS, BUT YOU WOULD NOT WANT TO MESS WITH A KING COBRA—ONE SINGLE BITE CAN KILL A FULLY GROWN ELEPHANT. IF YOU FIND YOURSELF IN A WOODED AREA IN HIS NATIVE SOUTHEAST ASIA, YOU WOULD BE ADVISED TO WATCH YOUR STEP.

### MONTY "BUZZER" MOSQUITO

#### DO NOT APPROACH

ABOUT 1 MILLION DEATHS A YEAR FROM MOSQUITO-BORNE MALARIA

BELIEVE IT OR NOT, THIS TINY CRITTER IS THE MOST DANGEROUS ANIMAL ON THE PLANET. DO NOT BE DECEIVED BY ITS LACK OF SHARP TEETH OR KILLER CLAWS—THIS PARASITE FEEDS ON HUMAN BLOOD, SPREADING DEADLY DISEASES SUCH AS MALARIA FROM PERSON TO PERSON. THE MERCILESS MOSQUITO IS BELIEVED TO BE AT LARGE IN TROPICAL REGIONS AROUND THE WORLD.

# MEET THE MOB

## "SLASHER" SHARK
### RESPONSIBLE FOR UP TO 100 ATTACKS A YEAR

THIS GANG MEMBER MAY NOT BE THE BRAINS OF THE OPERATION, BUT A SHARK'S SENSES ARE SECOND TO NONE; SPECIAL SENSORY CELLS ALLOW IT TO DETECT ELECTRICAL SIGNALS EMITTED BY THE SMALLEST OF MOVEMENTS. SO, IF YOU FIND YOURSELF IN A SHARK'S TERRITORY, DON'T MOVE A MUSCLE! THE MOST FEARED OF THIS SPECIES, THE GREAT WHITE SHARK, IS A FORMIDABLE PREDATOR AND CAN SNIFF OUT ONE PART OF BLOOD IN ONE MILLION PARTS OF WATER.

## "TOXIC" JELLYFISH
### VENOMOUS STING KILLS MORE THAN 100 SWIMMERS EVERY YEAR

THIS FASCINATING CREATURE MAY LOOK DELICATE, BUT LOOKS CAN BE VERY DECEIVING. THE DEADLY BOX JELLYFISH HAS AN EXTREMELY FAST-WORKING TOXIN AND KILLS MORE PEOPLE EACH YEAR THAN ANY OTHER MARINE ANIMAL. A SINGLE BOX JELLYFISH CAN HAVE AS MANY AS 16 TENTACLES, EACH ABOUT 10 FT (3 M) LONG AND COVERED IN STINGERS. THESE TOXIC CREATURES ARE TRANSPARENT AND DIFFICULT TO SPOT, BUT THEY HANG OUT MOSTLY IN AUSTRALIA.

## "CRUSHER" ELEPHANT
### MORE THAN 600 PEOPLE EVERY YEAR TRAMPLED UNDERFOOT

NOT EVERY ELEPHANT IS A GENTLE GIANT. THEY ARE THE WORLD'S LARGEST LAND MAMMALS AND, WEIGHING UP TO 6.6 TONS (6 TONNES), ARE THE HEAVIEST OF THE ANIMAL KINGDOM. THEIR AMPLE BULK COULD CRUSH THE STRONGEST OPPOSITION. AS ONE OF THE MOST DANGEROUS ANIMALS IN AFRICA AND ASIA, ELEPHANTS CAN BECOME VERY AGGRESSIVE AND ATTACK WITHOUT WARNING. IF THIS HAPPENS, A QUICK CLIMB UP THE NEAREST TREE MAY JUST SAVE YOU.

## "SNAPPER" CROCODILE
### LIKELY TO SNAP UP ABOUT 2,000 PEOPLE EVERY YEAR

CUNNINGLY DISGUISED AS A LOG, THE CROCODILE CAN LAY STILL IN THE WATER FOR HOURS ON END. THEN IT WILL LUNGE, PULLING ITS VICTIM UNDER THE WATER WITH ITS POWERFUL JAWS AND DROWNING IT. A HUNGRY CROC WILL EAT MONKEYS, SNAKES, CATTLE, OR HUMANS—WHATEVER COMES ITS WAY. MOST OF THESE KILLING MACHINES LURK IN RIVERS AND LAKES, SO BEST CHECK WHERE YOU SWIM. THE MOST AGGRESSIVE CROCS ARE LOCATED IN SOUTHEAST ASIA, AFRICA, AND AUSTRALIA.

## "CLAWS" BIG CAT
### HIS KIND MAUL TO DEATH ABOUT 250 PEOPLE EVERY YEAR

WITH THEIR GIANT, TERRIFYING FANGS, SHARP CLAWS, AND LIGHTNING SPEED, BIG CATS—LIONS, TIGERS, LEOPARDS, AND JAGUARS—ARE PERFECT HUNTERS. IF YOU COME ACROSS A LION IN AFRICA OR INDIA, YOU JUST HAVE TO HOPE IT'S NOT HUNGRY. BECAUSE ONCE YOU ARE IN HIS SIGHTS, ESCAPE IS UNLIKELY. THE BEST THING THAT YOU CAN DO IS TO STAY STILL AND TRY TO LOOK BIG AND SCARY. ABOVE ALL, SHOW NO FEAR.

## "STINGER" SCORPION
### DEADLY STING IS RESPONSIBLE FOR UP TO 5,000 FATALITIES A YEAR

MOST SCORPION STINGS ARE NO WORSE THAN A BEE'S, BUT BEWARE THE NORTH AFRICAN DEATHSTALKER SCORPION. ITS STINGERS CONTAIN A POWERFUL VENOM THAT CAUSES INTENSE PAIN, FEVER, PARALYSIS, AND, IN THE WORST CASES, DEATH. A STING FROM A DEATHSTALKER IS USUALLY NOT ENOUGH TO KILL SOMEONE, BUT UNLESS YOU WANT A NASTY NIP, IT'S STILL WORTH CHECKING INSIDE YOUR SHOES!

# SHARK ATTACK

Do sharks deserve their status as serial killers of the sea? Or are they simply confused and misunderstood creatures that don't even like the way we taste? Are they devastatingly deadly hunters that plan every detail of their attacks? Or do they just happen to be swimming near us with their mouths open, then, whoops, chompfest? You decide!

## USUAL SUSPECTS

It's a fact: of the 375 different species of sharks, only about 15 percent live in coastal waters or shallow depths where people might encounter them. That cuts the peril potential down quite a lot. Only four species have been responsible for the vast majority (85 percent) of attacks. They are the great white, tiger, bull, and oceanic whitetip. Other sharks just aren't big or powerful enough to kill us, although they certainly can bite!

*HEY! STOP SNACKING ON DEFENSELESS TOURISTS! WHAT DO YOU HAVE TO SAY FOR YOURSELVES?*

**SHARK SCHOOL**

*OKAY, PUPS, THIS IS HOW WE DO IT. JUST WATCH AND LEARN.*

*ARRGH!*

*I SAY, THIS ISN'T MY USUAL FISH DINNER. IT TASTES LIKE CHICKEN.*

*IMAGINE BUMPING INTO YOU! OF ALL THE SEAS IN THE WORLD, YOU HAD TO SWIM INTO MINE.*

*HELP!*

*YOU JUST LIE THERE, WHILE I LIE LOW... AND THEN, BANG! I ATTACK. SNEAKY!*

*JUST EVENING OUT THE ODDS: HUMANS KILL 20–30 MILLION OF US A YEAR THROUGH COMMERCIAL AND SPORTFISHING.*

## THREE TYPES OF ATTACKS

In a bump-and-bite offensive, the shark circles its victim (perhaps a survivor of a plane crash or shipwreck), bumps into them with its sandpaper-rough skin, and then takes a big bite. The shark may continue to bump and bite until it has bumped the (former) survivor off. Hit-and-run attacks are common in shallow waters near the shore. The shark, hunting for something else, zooms in and takes a chunk out of a human leg or foot. It often decides that the human has no taste and swims away. In deep waters, a shark can simply appear out of nowhere in a sneaky surprise!

## ATTACK STATS

There are about 30 to 50 unprovoked shark attacks a year worldwide. Even in the year with the most recorded shark attacks (2000), there were only 79 attacks, just 11 of which were fatal to their victims.

## GREAT WHITE GARBAGE DISPOSAL

Sharks seem willing to swallow just about anything—it has even been suggested that some sharks swallow these objects for ballast. Some of the things reportedly found in sharks caught at various times and places include: an almost whole reindeer, three bottles of beer, a handbag, a wristwatch, a full-grown spaniel dog, and the headless body of a man dressed in a suit of armor.

## IN FOR THE KRILL

The bigger the shark, the badder the bite, right? Not true. Actually, you have nothing to fear from the very largest sharks—the whale shark and the basking shark. These gigantic filter feeders swim along with their mouths agape, sifting enormous amounts of krill, plankton, small fish, and squids from the water.

## JAWS OF DEATH

Multiple rows of sharp, serrated triangular teeth are packed inside a shark's crushingly powerful jaws. And the teeth are constantly replaced as they fall out! With just one bite, a shark can pull away a huge chunk of flesh, or completely sever a human limb. Advantage: shark.

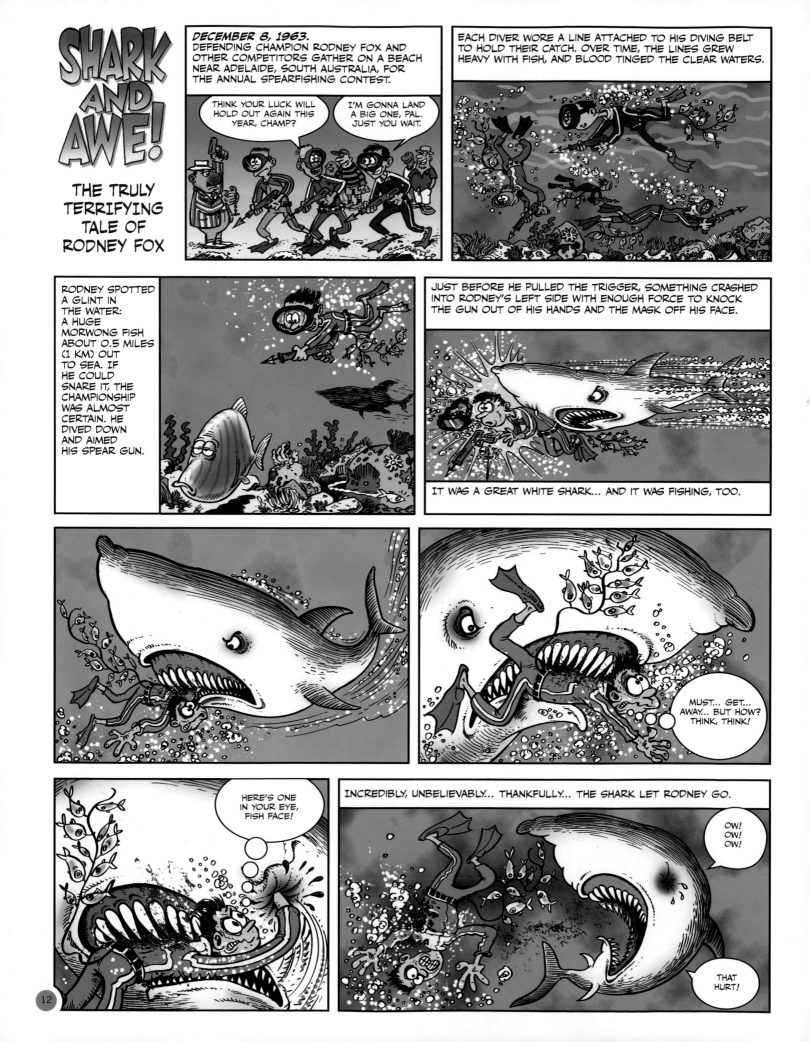

RODNEY WAS FREE! NOW HE HAD TO GET OUT OF THE KILLING ZONE. HE THRUST HIS ARM OUT IN SELF-DEFENSE BUT PLUNGED IT RIGHT BACK INTO THE SHARK'S MOUTH, WHICH WAS FULL OF GIANT RAZORLIKE TEETH THAT RIPPED THE FLESH FROM HIS HANDS AND FOREARMS.

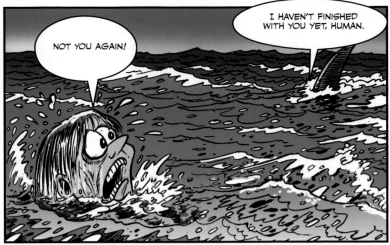

THE SHARK CLAMPED ITS JAWS SHUT AROUND THE LINE OF FISH STILL ATTACHED TO RODNEY'S BELT. THEN, IT PLUNGED INTO DEEPER WATERS, PULLING RODNEY ALONG WITH IT. HIS BODY SPINNING, HIS HANDS WORKING AT THE LINE ATTACHMENT, RODNEY WAS CERTAIN HE WAS BEING DRAGGED TO HIS DOOM.

SNAP! SUDDENLY THE LINE BROKE. RODNEY STRUGGLED TO THE SURFACE, WOOZY FROM HIS WOUNDS. HIS ATTACKER SWAM ON INTO THE WATERY DEPTHS, IN SEARCH OF ANOTHER VICTIM.

SOME FRIENDS ON A NEARBY BOAT ROWED TO THE RESCUE, DRAGGING RODNEY ONBOARD. HE WAS A WRECK. HIS RIB CAGE WAS CRUSHED, HIS LUNG WAS RIPPED OPEN, AND HIS ABDOMEN, SPLEEN, AND THE MAIN ARTERY FROM HIS HEART WERE EXPOSED. HIS WETSUIT WAS THE ONLY THING THAT WAS HOLDING HIM TOGETHER!

RODNEY WAS RUSHED TO THE NEAREST HOSPITAL, WHERE THE SURGEONS WORKED TO REASSEMBLE HIS BROKEN BODY. FOUR HOURS AND 462 STITCHES LATER, THE SURGICAL TEAM HAD SAVED HIS LIFE.

RODNEY HAD SURVIVED A FEROCIOUS SHARK ATTACK. TO REMIND HIM OF HIS ORDEAL, HE WORE THE SCAR OF THE SHARK'S BITE, AND PART OF THE SHARK'S TOOTH WAS EMBEDDED IN HIS WRIST BONE. AS IF HE COULD EVER FORGET...

AFTER A FEW MONTHS, RODNEY WAS DIVING AGAIN. EAGER TO LEARN MORE ABOUT THE AWESOME ADVERSARY THAT ALMOST ENDED HIS LIFE, HE DESIGNED THE FIRST UNDERWATER OBSERVATION CAGE TO ALLOW DIVERS TO STUDY SHARKS UP CLOSE IN SAFETY.

RODNEY FOX IS CONSIDERED A WORLD AUTHORITY ON THE GREAT WHITE SHARK, AND EVEN THOUGH ONE PARTICULAR SHARK TRIED TO MAKE HIM EXTINCT, HE IS LEADING THE FIGHT TO SAVE THEM FROM EXTINCTION.

# FIGHT OR FLIGHT?

Hello, boys and girls! My name is Little Red Riding Hood, and I'm about to skip through the woods with a basket of goodies to take to my grandmother's cottage. What's that you say? Maybe I should mail them instead? Nonsense! I've traipsed through this magical forest countless times, and no harm has ever come my way. Ignore those silly warnings about killer animals. What could possibly go wrong for me, or my muffins? Off we go…

## FALCON

Hey, birdbrain! Bet you think you're going to swoop down and get those razor-sharp talons into this red riding hood, or puncture me with that sharp beak. I know you're just defending your territory… I'll duck into the forest so that I'm harder to single out. I'm not going to panic or run, but I'll stare right into your beady eyes.

## POLAR BEAR

Mister Polar Bear, you sure are a long way from home, but I know what to do. I'll stare at the bear as I back away slowly to a safe shelter. That cape trick to look bigger might come in handy. Grandma won't mind if I drop a few muffins as I retreat. The bear might stop and sniff them, buying me a little extra time.

## BEWARE OF THE ANIMALS

## MOUNTAIN LION

I'd be lying if I didn't admit that you, lion, are a tiny bit scary. I'll stay calm and steady as I walk backward and stand up tall and straight while talking to the lion in a normal voice so that it understands that I am not a threat. I might just hold my red cape up over my head to make me look bigger. In a cat attack, it's better to fight back than run away.

## CHEETAH

You might look like a super-bad kitty, but I know you won't attack unless you are protecting your cubs, and I don't see any of those around. You're also not as fiercely armed in the claws-and-jaws department as, say, a lion. My best bet is to stand still, look you in the eye, and either back up or wait for you to pad away. There you go. Good kitty.

## BEAR

Almost there, and there's a bear. Think, Red! I need to look right into its eyes, and I may just have to dump these muffins to save my own buns. I'll move back and make sure not to even try to outrun it or climb up a tree. I might play dead, curling up into a ball to protect my stomach, throat, and head. Once it leaves me alone, I'll make a run for it to Grandma's.

## GIANT SQUID

Sheesh! Grandma really needs to think about moving to the big city. Look at you, you creepy carnivorous calamari. The fact that you have a mouthful of sharp teeth in that beak does not concern me. You bite humans only in self-defense. So the best thing I can do is keep walking. And don't even think about squirting my cape with ink... I just had it dry-cleaned.

## MUSK OX

Now, this is getting ridiculous. Grandma taught me that musk oxen defend themselves by herding together with their sharp, pointy horns displayed. It's not natural for them to attack humans, unless we get too close. So I'm just going to take a shortcut around Mr. Musk Ox so that I don't end up skewered like a kebab.

## DOLPHIN

With permanent grins on their friendly faces, dolphins chatter to one another as they play in the waves. But there is a flip side to Flipper: bottlenose dolphins have been known to kill their own babies and for no known reason hunt down porpoises, beat them to death, and then play with their corpses. Maybe they just flip out.

## KOALA

With their velvety rounded bodies and tufty ears, these treetop dwellers are the very picture of cuteness. However, notice the not-so-cute claws, made for stripping tough tree leaves and clambering up branches. If provoked, they will use them to shred your skin. They also have a nasty bite that doesn't bear thinking about.

## SLOW LORIS

Its cartoon-huge eyes and furry body are adorable to behold, but the slow loris is capable of pulling a fast one. It secretes a toxin on its inner elbows and then mixes it up with its saliva. When it bites, it injects this toxic spit, causing horrible stomach pains and sometimes even death.

# CUTE OUTFIT, NASTY SURPRISE

Awwwww! Look at this adorable assortment of animals. Wouldn't you like to take one home to love forever? Think again, as each of these charming critters has a teeny-tiny secret: it can attack, maim, and even kill. They may be cuddly and be begging you to pick them up and give them a big hug, but danger is their middle name. No matter how irresistible these animals appear to be, resist them.

## KINKAJOU

This sweetie is nicknamed "honey bear" for its rich golden fur and its habit of dipping its tongue into nectar. When it sleeps, it wraps its long tail around itself like a fluffy blanket. But if you startle a kinkajou, it may let out a horrendous scream before clawing your flesh and biting your skin. Honey, that's not funny.

## PANDA

With black-ringed eyes, a big round face, and an adorable chubby, fuzzy body, a panda looks just as cuddly as a toy version of itself. If you make a panda angry, though, get ready for pandemonium. Like other bears, it has a vicious bite and a scratch that can tear the skin from your bones.

## SKUNK

Bright-eyed and bushy-tailed the striped skunk may be, but if it aims its bottom your way, hightail it out of there. A skunk can spray a toxic cocktail of smelly chemicals from a pair of glands near its anus that can temporarily blind you, and the stinky stench can make you vomit.

## SWAN

When these beautiful birds glide up to their partners, the curves in their necks match to form a heart shape. Yet serene can turn to mean in an instant, especially if a swan's babies are threatened. They can strike people with their huge heavy wings and snip them with their sharp beaks.

## PLATYPUS

The platypus, with a duck bill, otter feet, and a beaver tail on a furry body, is an odd combination of cute and ugly. And it is certainly capable of some fairly ugly behavior: when a male platypus kicks its enemies, hollow spurs in its legs release a poison that is strong enough to kill small animals and cause humans months of agonizing muscle spasms.

## OTTER

Darting through river waters, these sleek critters appear to play all day, but during the mating season they like to play rough. The aggressive males can attack and kill pet dogs, gnawing at them with their teeth. You otter stay away from them.

# NIGHT STALKERS

Why are so many animals active at night? In hot places, it makes sense to hunt at night when it's cooler. Other animals may choose to prowl under the cover of darkness when there is less competition for food. Nocturnal animals generally have excellent senses of hearing and smell, and their eyes can adapt to see in the dimmest light. Meet some of the predators that go bump in the night… and find out why it's a good idea not to bump into them!

## 1. Tarantula

This teacup-size terror doesn't trap its prey in a web like other spiders. Instead, it creeps around at night and grabs frogs, toads, mice—even birds—with its horrid hairy legs, injects its prey with paralysing venom, and then bites it with its fangs to finish the job.

## 2. Jaguar

Stalking silently through the trees, this fearsome and ferocious big cat uses its sharp hearing to detect prey (deer, capybaras, and tapirs). Then, the jaguar pounces on its unfortunate victim. A jaguar's bite is so strong that it can crush through the skull of its prey to pierce the brain.

## 3. Green anaconda

The largest snake in the world, this South American slitherer can grow up to 29 ft (8.8 m) long and 1 ft (30 cm) in diameter. It gets that big by feeding on wild pigs, deer, birds, turtles, and jaguars. This snake coils its huge body around its prey and squeezes, suffocating its victim.

## 4. Owl

This silent hunter feeds on mice, shrews, and other small mammals. Special wing feathers muffle the sound of its approach so that it takes victims by surprise. Superior eyesight helps owls locate prey—some owls can hunt in complete darkness, relying on sound to guide them to their prey.

## 5. Natterer's bat

This expert night hunter finds its prey through echolocation. This means that it makes a high-pitched noise through its mouth or nose as it flies. Then, it listens to the echo that returns, figuring out the exact location of the prey, its size, and what direction it's moving in.

## 6. Red-eyed tree frog

Native to Central American rainforests, these frogs sleep by day, hidden among the foliage. At night, they hunt insects to eat. If a predator approaches, they pop their blood-red eyes and flash their huge orange feet to startle it while they make their escape.

### 7. Common brushtail possum

Possums are cat-size marsupials that feed at night on insects, fruit, spiders, tree nectar, and seeds. Although many are quiet, the common brushtail possum makes an unpleasant hissing call. Some possums carry bovine tuberculosis, which can damage a cow's lungs and lead to death.

### 8. White-bellied pangolin

Rows of overlapping scales—a bit like human fingernails—cover this mammal's body. At night, it sniffs out termite and ant nests, rips into them with its sharp claws, and licks up the insects with its sticky tongue, swallowing them whole. If attacked, it rolls into a ball.

### 9. Skunk

At dusk, skunks leave their shared dens to forage in the forests for food. They sniff around for a trace of food and then dig up a meal of mice, rats, fallen birds' eggs, insects, and fruit and nuts. Skunks may roll caterpillars on the ground to remove their hairs before eating them.

### 10. Spectacled bear

This South American bear is named for the cream-colored rings around its eyes. During the day, spectacled bears sleep in "tree houses," which they build by placing a row of sticks high up in the treetops. At night, they use these platforms to reach fruit and leaves.

# BLOOD SUCKERS!

Be afraid...be very afraid. These creepy creatures thirst for the blood of other animals, including you. Piercing through skin and veins with their monstrous mouthparts, they suck or lap up the blood that sustains them, until they must feed again. Watch out, or you might be their next victim!

## Fleas

These wingless insects, which can leap 200 times their own body length onto their victims, have thin bodies to maneuver through fur or hair. Fleas pierce your skin with hollow mouthparts and suck up a meal of blood, leaving behind a very itchy bite.

## Mosquitoes

Beware of the female of this species. Sensing the chemicals and heat that you give off, she lands on your skin and sticks in a sharp, thin proboscis. Her saliva stops your blood from clotting as she feeds, and her abdomen swells with your blood while you swell with a nasty itch.

## Bedbug

What living nightmares await you in your cozy bed? Lurking within the sheets or hiding out in tiny crevices, bedbugs launch their attack at night. With beaklike mouthparts, they suck up their fill of blood and can grow as large as apple seeds.

## Ticks

Waiting in tall grasses for a host to pass by, ticks stab their victims with pincerlike mandibles and tooth-covered feeding tubes. The teeth curve back on themselves to anchor the creatures into the host. After getting stuck in, they may feed for days until sated, but they can leave the host with more than just an itchy bite. Ticks carry a number of dangerous diseases, such as Lyme disease, from one host to another.

## Ambush bug

Master of disguise, the brightly colored ambush bug hides completely motionless on a flower. When its prey—such as a bee—comes near, the ambush bug strikes, using its thick front legs to capture the victim, paralysing it with toxins injected through its short beak. Finally, it sucks out the prey's blood and other bodily fluids.

## Vampire finch

Beware this blood-craving bird found in the flower nectar Beware this blood-craving bird found in the flower nectar such as flower at Beware this blood-craving bird found in the dry season, it pecks at Galápagos Islands. When food is in short supply during the dry season, it pecks at is in short until it bleeds and then sips the escaping a sea bird. Other finches line up to have a turn, and blood. Other bird finishes, the next one as soon as one bird finishes, the next one starts pecking.

Vampire bat

# STINGERS

Alert! Intruders are on the prowl, armed with sharp organs called stingers and extremely dangerous. Their lethal weapons are capable of piercing the skin of other animals to deliver venom—a toxic cocktail of nerve poisons and cell destroyers. Some stings may cause only momentary pain, but others are extremely potent, causing excruciating agony or even death.

## Portuguese man-of-war

With an air-filled, jellylike blue and pink body topped with a pink-ridged crest, this marine invertebrate trails very long 59-ft (18-m) tentacles behind it as it floats on the surface. Do not attempt to touch the tentacles as they contain a poison that is powerful enough to burn and blister your skin on contact.

## Cone snail

They may move at a snail's pace, but these reef-dwelling gastropods can pull a fast one. Cone snails shoot a harpoonlike tooth from an extendable "arm" into their chosen prey (often a fish) and release hundreds of toxins to paralyse it. Their sting is deadly to humans, and there is no known antivenin. Stay away!

## Honeybee

When a bee stings, the barbs at the end of its stinger catch in its victim's skin. The bee must leave its rear behind as it exits, but that is not the end of the pain: the stinger continues to pump venom—a mix of 40 various ingredients—for 10 minutes, and a pheromone is released to alert nearby bees to attack. Evade!

## Bullet ant

The pain from a South American bullet ant sting is likened to being shot with a gun. In fact, experts rate it among the most intense and excruciating sting of any insect. The agony lasts for three hours, along with nausea, cold sweats, and trembling. Gun it to get away!

## Tarantula hawk wasp

Pregnant wasps paralyse tarantulas with their stings then lay their eggs on the stunned spiders. When the babies hatch, they gobble up the spiders alive. Tarantula hawk wasps rarely sting humans, which is good news, as their sting is similar to being struck by lightning. Buzz off!

## Stingray

Equipped with one or more sharp serrated barbs on their tails, stingrays strike out when attacked. These fish spew vile venom through a painful puncture wound, causing instant agony. Although they're not aggressive to humans, they may sting if you step on them.

## Scorpion

There are thousands of scorpions, although most are harmless to humans. However, a few have a serious sting in their curving tails. Their venom sends pain radiating from the sting site throughout the body, causing numbness, twitching, breathing problems, and nausea. Hightail it away!

## Asian giant hornet

A sting from this thumb-size beast feels like having a hot nail driven into your skin, but it's the venom that really bugs you. Strong enough to dissolve human tissue and packed with pain-stimulating chemicals that shoot through the nervous system, the toxins can (and do) cause death.

# POISON PERILS

Here's a jarring thought: there are thousands of different poisonous animals out there. These creatures have a toxin in their glands or skin that can kill or sicken any animal that tries to nibble, sniff, or touch them. The poison attacks the nervous system or stops the heart and lungs from working. Poisonous animals are often brightly colored, so take the hint and stay away.

## Hooded pitohui

This family of strikingly colorful orange and black birds from New Guinea feeds on toxic beetles. As a result, neurotoxins build up in their skin and feathers. If a snake or bird of prey pounces, the toxin-laced feathers instantly repel it, causing numbness and tingling.

## Flamboyant cuttlefish

These odd-looking fish found in the seas of Australia and Indonesia stroll along the ocean floor with their arms, looking for dinner. Cuttlefish can change color in an instant to camouflage themselves when stalking their prey. To keep themselves safe from other predators, their muscle tissue contains a sickeningly strong poison.

## Stonefish

Lying on the seabed, stonefish are armed with spines on their backs to protect themselves from predators, such as sharks and rays. Should a predator pounce, they shoot out poison, causing paralysing pain. Stone me!

## Cane toad

Sensing danger, the cane toad begins to "cry," oozing out a white fluid from glands near its eyes and along its back. Contact with this milky poison causes twitching, limb collapse, breathing problems, then cardiac arrest. So don't kiss a tearful toad to make it feel better or you will feel much, much worse.

## Monarch butterfly

As larvae (an early stage of growth), these beautiful butterflies feed on the milkweed plant, from which they extract a supply of heart-stopping poison called glycoside. Come snacktime, birds that take a nibble of a monarch will soon learn that it is poisonous when they vomit it up. But this won't stop some birds, such as black-beaked orioles, which have a greater tolerance to the monarch's chemical defenses.

## Puss moth caterpillar

The puss moth larva is covered in long, lush locks of hairlike fur that conceal a nasty surprise: underneath, there are hollow, quill-like spines connected to sacs of pure poison. Any contact with the caterpillar releases the toxin, causing searing pain, itching, and headaches.

## Sea cucumber

When in danger, the sea cucumber expels a special organ loaded with toxins from its posterior. In the water, the organ splits into sticky toxic tubes that attach to the attacker, weakening its muscles and making it helpless. The poison can also cause permanent blindness if it gets into the eyes. Not to be used in salads!

## Poison-arrow frog

One of the world's most poisonous animals, the poison-arrow frog can kill a human with an amount of toxin equal to only two or three grains of table salt. Native to Central and South America, it secretes the poison through its skin. This terrifying toxin paralyses muscles and lungs, causing death.

## Fire salamander

When a predator gets ahold of it, this colorful newt releases a milky toxin from pores around its head and along both sides of its spine. The poison causes muscle convulsions and attacks the heart and lungs. Newt good.

## KILLER WHALES

The largest type of dolphin, killer whales earn their nickname, "wolves of the sea," by ganging up in pods to hunt. They sneak up on schools of fish and marine mammals, communicating with one another with almost silent calls that are undetectable to their victims. Killer whales attack from all sides to make a kill, then they share the catch of the day.

## BARRACUDA

Wolves of the sea, meet the "tigers of the ocean." Barracuda are natural-born killers equipped with a mouthful of fanglike teeth and huge appetites. When these fierce fish hunt in a group, they herd their prey together and then ram into their victims with a sudden burst of speed, snapping off chunks of fish flesh.

## ARMY ANTS

These ants live in huge colonies of up to 700,000 individuals. When they hunt, a regiment of up to 200,000 ants overwhelm their victims, including other ants or large arthropods, in an attack called a swarm raid. They chop up the flesh of their dead prey with machete-sharp jaws. It's no picnic.

# SWARM!

Many animals prefer prowling for their victims in groups. A pack of hunters can sometimes do a better job of bringing down prey than a single animal, especially if their target is a large one. A pack is also likely to confuse the victim. Other animals hunt in swarms or gangs because they live in extended families and do most things together.

## HONEYBEES

When thousands of buzzing bees pour out of a hive to swirl in the air like an angry striped cloud, they aren't coming after you… they're just moving to a new house. Bees swarm when they run out of honey storage space. The queen bee and the gang may swarm on a tree branch while bee scouts look for a good place to build a new hive.

## AFRICAN WILD DOGS

Roaming the plains and woodlands of Africa in a family pack, these wild dogs have colorful markings, unique to each dog, that help them spot one another. They hunt together in a deadly gang. A group of up to 20 dogs cooperates to tackle and bring down their much larger prey. Their bites are much worse than their barks.

## HARRIS'S HAWKS

Although many birds of prey hunt alone, these birds work together to attack lizards, rabbits, large insects, and other birds. A few birds at a time may set off on patrol to look for prey until they eventually land dinner, which they share. In other cases, the hawks quietly surround their prey, and after one bird swoops in to startle it, the others attack.

## MORMON CRICKETS

When a million or more of these crickets get together in a huge gang, they are capable of destroying entire fields of crops and vegetables. The densely packed swarm stretches as far as the eye can see and covers 1 mile (1.6 km) a day, devouring every plant in their path. No one knows why they swarm, but they really do bug people.

## PIRANHAS

With wide mouths packed full of razor-sharp teeth that are capable of stripping flesh from bone, these fish are deadly enough individually. But when they get together, it's murder. In a feeding frenzy, they can devour their prey in seconds, ripping off one chunk of flesh after another. By swarming together in a group, they also deter their own predators.

# MONSTERS OF THE DEEP

Splash! A daring deep-sea diver ventures from the sunlit surface waters down through the darkened ocean depths. The quest: to find a long-lost chest of buried treasure. The diver descends even farther, searching for a glint of gold, but is unaware of the fate that awaits...for there in the waters lurks a gruesome gang of hideous undersea creatures. Dive in!

## OCEAN SUNFISH

Face it, I'm freaky. I look like a huge flattened fish head with a tail stuck onto it. I tip the scales at 2,200 lb (1,000 kg), and I'm as long as an adult human. As I often roam near the ocean's surface, that diver might get an early fright on the way down—but don't panic, I mostly eat jellyfish.

## CHIMERA FISH

Emeralds glinting from a treasure chest? Afraid not, sucker. You're looking at my oversize catlike eyes. Slippery skin covers my body, tapering to a ratlike tail. My dental plates are strong enough to munch on clams and crabs, shells and all, so keep your hands to yourself if you don't want to lose those fingers!

## VIPERFISH

I could scare that diver right out of his suit with my fearsome fangs. Maybe I'll swim straight into him as fast as I can, impaling his flesh on my terrible teeth. My hinged jaws enable me to swallow large prey whole...but something his size may be out of my depth.

## SPERM WHALE

When that diver gets a look at all 60 ft (20 m) and 55 tons (50 tonnes) of me, he's so gonna blubber. I can eat a ton (tonne) of fish and squids a day and still have room for dessert. Lucky for him, I don't have a taste for humans, although I may accidentally capsize boats that get in the way of my enormous tail.

## DANA OCTOPUS SQUID

Hey, diver! I may be shining like gold, but I'm not what you're seeking. I have a pair of lemon-size light-making organs called photophores on the ends of two arms. I can flash them on and off, making blindingly bright light to stun and disorient my prey.

## SEA LAMPREY

I have big reddish eyes and a mouth filled with a spiral of sharp teeth and a rasplike tongue. I'm a parasite, so I latch my mouth onto prey and stay there for days or even weeks, feeding on their blood and bodily fluids. You, diver, had better hope that I don't become too attached to you.

## MEGAMOUTH SHARK

A close encounter with me would make that diver's jaw drop—mine already did. The sight of my huge mouth and head is awesomely scary, but the real reason I'm opening wide is to filter food as I propel my bulky body through the ocean depths.

## FANGTOOTH FISH

Not far now, diver, but you need to get past me first. I may be little, but my mouth is stuffed with teeth. In proportion to my body, I have the biggest teeth of any fish. They don't even fit in my mouth, so pockets in the roof of my mouth fit the fangs on my lower jaw when it closes.

# HOW ABOUT A DIP?

Do you like to be beside the seaside? Be wary: there may be something in the waves. You don't have to go very far to wade into dangerous waters. A whole poolfull of potentially perilous creatures lurks just off the world's coastlines and riverbanks. They may seem relatively harmless, but they have been known to attack people without provocation. Take a look at some of the most beastly of these bathing beasts.

## HIPPOPOTAMUS

Found throughout sub-Saharan Africa, the horrible hippo has earned a terrible reputation for its vicious attacks. Its enormous bulk makes it a formidable foe, and it is surprisingly agile, able to tip over boats and munch the former occupants with its huge teeth. On land, a hippo can charge at you and swing its head like a hammer to bash you into oblivion.

## ELECTRIC EEL

Ready for a shock? This predator can stun its prey into submission by releasing a 600-volt burst of electricity. Organs on its body store electricity like batteries between attacks. An eel's shock is not actually powerful enough to kill a human outright, but you might suffer a heart attack or drown in the aftermath.

## WEEVER FISH

This small sand-colored fish is not a great swimmer. Instead, it lies buried on the seabed with just a fin sticking out until something tasty swims by. If you should step on a weever fish, its spines will pump venom into your foot. A sizzle of pure pain will shoot through your body as your foot turns red and swells up like a foot-shaped balloon.

## FLOWER SEA URCHIN

Small and spiny, these creatures make their way across the bottom of a tidal pool munching on algae. Some of their spines are capable of releasing venom as they pinch their prey, presenting a prickly problem: the venom causes extreme pain and can lead to death. Blooming awful.

## CATFISH

There are more than 1,600 venomous species of these finned fatales. Venom glands are located alongside their bony spines. When defending itself from attack, the killer catfish locks its spines into place, stabs its predator, and releases its terrible toxins into the open wound. Bad kitty!

## SEA SNAKE

An aquatic relation of the cobra, this slippery customer lives in the shallows, feeding on fish and eel and popping up for a gulp of air from time to time. If provoked, it may sink its venom-laced fangs into your leg. In a matter of minutes, your muscles stiffen, your jaw spasms, your vision is blurry, and you struggle to breathe.

## BLUE-RINGED OCTOPUS

Do not disturb this rock-pool dweller. If you do step on it or pick it up, someone is going to get hurt. Its bite isn't painful, but its saliva carries a venom powerful enough to kill—and there is no antivenin. Within minutes, you feel woozy, your vision dims, your senses of touch and speech disappear, and you stop breathing as paralysis sets in.

## CRENULATED FIRE CORAL

This yellowish pore-covered sea coral branches out on reefs or attaches itself to walls, cement pilings, or other solid objects under the water. There is only one thing you need to know about it: reef it alone. Should you touch it, your skin will burn and erupt in a painful, blistery rash.

# POISONOUS PLANTS

Step inside our little shop of horrors. While vegetation helps to sustain life on Earth, there are flowers, trees, shrubs, and even hedges out there that can kill. Some are dangerous to touch, while others are toxic if swallowed or inhaled. Nasty reactions range from irritation to death. Why are some plants poisonous? It's simply their defense against being eaten. The stories of these green meanies will have you rooted to the spot.

## Manchineel tree ▶

This resembles an apple tree, but the fruit are nicknamed "apples of death." Eating the fruit causes blistering in the mouth and throat, and can be fatal. The tree leaks a milky white sap that can blister the skin, while smoke from a burning tree causes blindness. This is one bad apple tree.

## Nightshade ▲

Also known as belladonna or the devil's cherry, the leaves and berries of this plant contain atropine—a deadly chemical compound. A snack-size portion of berries causes slurred speech, blurred vision, horrible headaches, breathing problems, and convulsions. That's not berry nice.

## Castor bean ▶

These brutal beans contain the deadliest plant poison on Earth: ricin. Just a handful of beans contain enough of this poison to kill an adult within a few minutes. Even harvesting the plant can give a person nerve damage. Do not serve baked.

## ▼ Doll's eyes

Named after its startling appearance, the entire plant is poisonous but the berries pack a particular punch. If you pop an eye into your mouth, the poison relaxes heart muscle tissue, leading to cardiac arrest and death—all in the blink of an eye.

## Rosary pea ▲

Pea-shaped pods along this vine split open when dry to reveal bright red pealike seeds. Popping a few peas leads to drooling, vomiting, a high temperature, convulsions, seizures, and may eventually cause death. You most definitely must mind these Ps.

## Larkspur ▶

These blue-purple plants are popular in gardens, but they are packed with alkaloids. A nibble on the leaves and flowers brings intense burning of the mouth and throat, a feeling of lightheaded confusion, severe headaches, vomiting, and, at worst, suffocation.

## Water hemlock ▶

This relative of the parsnip is extremely poisonous. The toxins—concentrated in the roots, but also found in the leaves and stems—act so quickly that there may be no time for treatment. Touching hemlock can cause a reaction, but should you ingest it, expect grand mal seizures, loss of consciousness, violent muscle contractions, and possible death. Stick to its harmless relative.

## ◀ Narcissus

Are daffodils a delightful sign of spring or toxic killers? Both! The onionlike bulbs are the enemies, not the flowers. The bulbs contain a strong poison that can numb the nervous system and paralyse heart muscle with deadly consequences.

# PRECARIOUS PLANET

Get ready for some cataclysmic events: fires, floods, volcanoes, and earthquakes are all in the cards. Watch out for wild winds and freak rains of frogs, and keep away from hostile places. From icy wastes to scorching deserts, climates can kill, so it's not the end of the world if they're changing... or is it?

## Who wears the pants?

You come across British adventurer Conrad Dickinson's frozen underpants, which he wore for 70 days in a row on his trek to the South Pole in 2005. Quickly move on a space to avoid the stench!

The endless night of the Arctic winter drives you crazy. Miss a turn while you stare mindlessly at the northern lights.

# FINISH

You're trying to walk against icy katabatic winds (strong winds that come down from mountains) blowing at speeds of up to 199 mph (320 km/h). Forget it. You're blown back two spaces.

Another team has reached the Pole first. Aaaargh! Before returning the way you came, miss two turns weeping salty tears over all that pain and suffering for nothing.

You're seeing islands hovering in the distance like fairy-tale castles. Relax—it's just a mirage. But miss a turn while you pitch a tent and get some rest—you need it.

Crack! The ice sheet you're walking along is breaking up. You're now stuck on an iceberg drifting out to sea. Miss a turn while you paddle back to the mainland.

## Dig this

Miss a turn while you dig out British explorer August Courtauld from his tent on the Greenland icecap—he's been stuck in there for six months during a weather-observation mission in 1931 after leaving his snow shovel outside one night.

Polar bear alert! Your only hope of not becoming bear food is to play dead and curl up into a ball to protect your face and neck. Miss a turn until the bear has lost interest in you.

# BASE CAMP

The air at the poles is biting cold and dry as can be. Time for a water stop. Miss a turn while you rehydrate.

# ICE RACE!

Throw the dice to dash across the coldest, driest, windiest place on Earth and reach the finish pole first. May the best team win. Better not shake on it—at -58°F (-50°C), drop a glove and your hand will freeze solid in minutes. All set? On your mark, get set, go!

Don some goggles to cut out the glare from the white snow. You'll avoid getting snowblind, and you'll look cool, too! Move on an extra space.

## Once bitten...

Danish explorer Peter Freuchen's tootsies are badly frostbitten on the Canadian Arctic mapping mission of 1923. Do you: a) agree to the Inuit healer who has kindly offered to bite them off or b) bash them off with a hammer? If you answered b), you're correct. Throw again.

Ouch! Vicious jaegers are attacking your head with their feet. Move ahead two spaces while you dash for cover from these sea-bird bullies.

You take a sip from an Arctic lake—without realizing it's also a toilet for local beavers. A nasty little bug gives you the dreaded "beaver fever." Miss a turn while you recover. You'll stay warm with all that running to the toilet you'll be doing.

A leopard seal tries to drag you off the ice and into the water. Miss a turn while you wrench yourself free of those fearsome jaws.

Temperatures have plummeted. Put on an extra layer, wipe away your frozen snot, and hurry on two spaces to keep your blood circulating.

You've slipped into the dark, icy Arctic waters. Throw again to get out before you turn into a human ice cube.

You're in luck—an Inuit family takes a shine to you and wraps you up in some of their thick fur clothes. Those snowshoes are great, too. Snug and warm, move on three spaces.

## Sweet dreams

You've tripped over the four iron beds left by Italian mountaineer the Duke of Abruzzi on his 1897 expedition to Alaska. Miss a turn while you fantasize about having a warm blanket.

## It's a dog's life

Rations are running low. On the first expedition that reached the South Pole in 1912, Danish leader, Roald Amundsen, decides that there's nothing to do but to cook up some husky casserole. Half the expedition's dogs are killed. With a full belly but a heavy heart, move on two spaces.

There's no better way to speed across the ice than with a team of huskies and a sled. Mush! Move speedily on two spaces.

# SAVAGE SEAS

Ahoy there, landlubbers! While you splash around in your blissful bath, spare a thought for those who spend their lives on the ocean waves. The sea is full of nasty surprises: one day it is dead calm, the next it is a seething cauldron. Mountainous waves can toss a small craft to and fro or leave a giant tanker high and dry. If you hear sailors' tales of Davy Jones's locker, icebergs, fog, and fire, take heed! One day you, too, could find yourself in stormy waters...

## All at sea

Winds and currents are the powerful elements that are scarily in control of a vessel's movements on the open sea, with large waves tossing ships around as if they're toys—a nightmare for any seasick-prone sailor. Without adequate protection and with the Sun's rays being reflected by the water's surface, exposed skin can suffer painful sunburn and the eyes can become bloodshot and swollen.

## Wild waves

At sea, there is nowhere to hide from howling winds or giant waves that can send a ship the size of a small town to the ocean floor in about 12 seconds. In 1995, the luxury liner *Queen Elizabeth II* survived being hit by a rogue wave, said to be a staggering 10 stories high!

## Whale tale

Rocks and underwater reefs aren't the only things to steer clear of at sea. Whales are fishy mammals, so they need to surface to breathe, which can bring them into contact with any vessels floating on the surface. In 1851, a sperm whale smashed into a whaling ship, sinking it in minutes.

## Iceberg ahead!

When the "unsinkable" ship *Titanic* hit a large iceberg on April 14, 1912, it sank in a few hours, killing 1,523 people. Icebergs are floating masses of ice, 90 percent of which is hidden beneath the sea's surface. So even small icebergs are more menacing than they look—floating just above the water's surface, they can be very hard to spot in fog.

## Shiver me timbers!

Unless you're in the balmy Caribbean, chances are you'll be in cold water. Icy seas will quickly numb the bones of even the hardiest sailor. Even in water of 50°F (10°C), you cannot survive more than three hours without a wetsuit or by huddling up to other crew members.

## Stormy times

In 1947, Norwegian adventurer Thor Heyerdahl set sail across the Pacific on a balsa-wood raft, called *Kon-Tiki*, using only ocean currents and the wind. When a violent storm flooded the raft, his crew survived on rainwater and flying fish that landed on deck.

## Into the abyss

The deeper you venture into the depths of the sea, the more the pressure builds, so submarines are built as strong as tanks so as not to be crushed. In 2005, the Russian submarine *Priz* was rescued after getting caught in fishnets 620 ft (190 m) below the surface. With a dwindling oxygen supply, the crew was lucky not to die from carbon-dioxide poisoning, which was the fate of 900 men aboard *Thetis* when it sank in 1939.

## Water shortage

As any sailor worth his salt will tell you, oceans are deserts. Drinking salty seawater just makes you thirstier and sick. In 2004, a current swept Vietnamese fisherman Bui Duc Phuc 62 miles (100 km) from shore. After drifting for days, he drank his own urine to stay alive. Chewing fish eyes or drinking turtle blood are other options. Yo, ho, ho!

# Bermuda Triangle

There are many stories of ships and aircraft that have mysteriously disappeared in the infamous Bermuda Triangle—an area of the Atlantic Ocean between Bermuda, Florida, and Puerto Rico. Whether you believe the spooky accounts of vessels, crews, and passengers vanishing without a trace or dismiss them as too-tall tales, these weird waters have a fearsome reputation.

## Crazy compasses

Some people claim that the Bermuda Triangle is an area where Earth's magnetic field is so uneven that a compass points true north (the geographical north pole) rather than magnetic north, leading to all sorts of navigational mix-ups. However, research suggests that this hasn't been the case since the 19th century, and so can't account for those disappearances that occurred in the 20th century.

## Horse latitudes

Sailors in the past relied on wind power to take them across the seas, with a real danger of becoming stranded midocean if the winds failed. A rotating ocean current—the North Atlantic Gyre—within the Bermuda Triangle could sweep a becalmed ship off course. The area was known as the horse latitudes because becalmed sailors would throw their horses overboard to conserve drinking water.

## Hurricanes and waterspouts

This part of the Atlantic is well known for its violent storms and sudden changes in weather. Waterspouts—tornadoes over the sea—are not uncommon, and a hurricane could easily swamp a ship or crash a plane. But would this make a vessel disappear without leaving any trace?

United States of America

Bermuda

## Rogue waves

For years, scientists dismissed the notion of freak waves smashing ships to pieces, but, in 1995, a wave detector on an oil rig in the North Sea recorded a huge 65-ft (20-m) wave. Could similar waves explain the disappearances in the Atlantic? It would take a real monster to sink a 22-000-ton (20,000-tonne) ship.

## Underwater eruptions

Some people have suggested that the sea simply opens and swallows up ships. Incredibly, this could actually happen. Large eruptions of methane gas on the seabed have been known to make oil rigs collapse. A passing ship would sink like a stone, and the methane could set fire to planes flying overhead.

## Snagged by seaweed

At the heart of the Bermuda Triangle lies the Sargasso Sea, named after the giant forest of sargassum seaweed that grows there. Old sailors' yarns tell of ships trapped for eternity in the choking mass of seaweed. In 1840, the French ship *Rosalie* was found here drifting, derelict—and deserted.

## Abductions

Caribbean waters have long been a favorite hunting ground for pirates, who may have sunk the vessels that were later reported missing after taking whatever they could find onboard. But what about the ships that were found without a crew and with their cargo intact? Some blame abductions by aliens. Beam me up, me hearties!

Florida

Cuba

Haiti

Jamaica

Puerto Rico

## Camel curves

If someone says you're built like a camel, take it as a compliment. This "ship of the desert" can go for days without a drink, while its fatty hump is tailor-made for the desert's two-week no-food diet. Gorgeous long eyelashes keep the sand out of the camel's eyes, while flat feet and tough soles make it the best mode of transportation on the scorching soft sand.

**SAND EXFOLIATION**

Removing a thin layer of dead cells from your skin can make it look healthy and radiant. So why not use the power of a desert sandstorm to give you that just-exfoliated look? But don't overdo it—sand moving at high speed can strip the paint off a car!

# DESERT SALON

The swelteringly hot desert is a barren place, full of hidden dangers and perilous pitfalls. The horrendous heat causes you to sweat out vital liquids, making you thirsty, tired, dizzy, and confused. But what is this tranquil oasis? Could it be a mirage? No, it's the deluxe Desert Salon. Time to relax and pamper yourself silly with one of the desert treatments on offer.

## Locust snacks

Got the munchies? Then dig into our scrumptious selection of snacks. Bite into a crunchy locust or tickle your tonsils by slipping a wiggly witchetty grub down your throat. Please note our bring-your-own-water policy—it's in short supply around here.

## Sight for six eyes

The tranquility of the desert is so relaxing. Just don't nod off. The sand spider has eyes only for you—all six of them. This critter likes to jump out on unsuspecting prey, and its cryotoxins are as deadly as they come.

TANNING BOOTH

CHILL-OUT ROOM

ACUPUNCTURE

WET ROOM

Sunken eyes and shriveled skin are so last year! Tan at your own pace by sheltering your body from the blistering desert sun. We recommend covering up bare skin and wearing dark glasses to protect your eyes from the glare, while a free Bedouin headscarf for all new clients will shield your head—and keep out the dust!

Need a break from the sweltering heat? No problem—just wait for sunset and feel the temperatures plummet to below freezing as the dry desert sand quickly loses its heat. Cool! Then just lie back on the dunes, close your eyes, and relax to the eerie singing and booming noises of the desert at night.

Keep bumping into a spiky cactus to get the full-body acupuncture treatment. Feel your aches and tension fade away as the spikes pierce your skin. Bliss! Even if you haven't made an appointment, the jumping cholla cactus has stems that fall off so easily that they will prick you as you pass by. A timesaving option.

When it rains in the desert, it really pours. Low-lying creek beds can turn into surging rivers in just a few minutes. How refreshing after a day in the hot sun. Make the most of it, but don't linger too long in the salty water found in many deserts—it can give you a nasty rash!

## Local wildlife

Watch and learn from these bad boys in our waiting room. It's all about encouraging rest and relaxation for this temperamental group. Observe how the usually fierce Gila monster takes it easy in the midday sun. Listen to the rattle of a rattlesnake's tail, but we recommend you leave him be—his venom is deadly. And although our scorpion has a nasty sting in its tail, it sure adds atmosphere at night when it glows in the dark under a UV light.

## Water cooler

An old Bedouin trick is to turn over half-buried stones in the desert just before the sun rises. Fine drops of water form on the stones' cool surfaces. Chilled water is just what you need on a hot day at the Desert Salon.

# JUNGLE PERILS!

Help! It's a jungle in here: hot, humid, and heaving with bugs. Getting lost is easy, as everything looks the same—green! Maps won't help, so your best bet is to take a guide. If you're alone, don't panic— here are the handiest hints to ensure you make it out alive…

## Tough terrain

Watch your step while navigating the jungle, as mud holes and quicksand can take you by surprise. Use a machete to chop through the thick undergrowth, but don't hack your leg off in the process! By the evening, happy campers should choose an area with care and avoid river beaches—if heavy rain falls overnight, your tent will be swept away.

## Hidden killers

Need to cool off? If you want to take a dip, check for alligator and caiman tracks where you choose to swim. These predators love to lurk near the water's edge. It's a similar story with hippos: they may look cuddly, but keep your distance—hippos are very territorial and will attack swimmers.

## Hothouse

Budding Tarzans should take it easy in the jungle. Nothing can prepare you for the heat and humidity, so don't push yourself too hard. As you move around the jungle, be sure to keep drinking. If you sweat more than you drink, you'll get dehydrated, and this can lead to severe heat stroke.

## Terrifying trees

If you're climbing trees for fruit, watch out for the many venomous snakes that like to hunt in the branches, including bushmasters, mambas, and boomslangs. They blend in with the bark and leaves, so look carefully. And if you're tired from all that climbing, don't nap under the trees, as falling deadwood kills more jungle novices than anything else.

## Pesky plants

There is a high risk of snagging your clothes or even your skin in the jungle. Long vines called "wait-awhiles" have sharp barbs that catch easily and slow you down. Even worse is the aptly named stinging tree: its large, heart-shaped leaves are covered in spikes. One touch and you'll get a nasty rash that lasts for months. Ouch!

## Bug watch

Boring-looking bugs bring the most trouble, so keep your wits about you and always use insect repellent. Small botflies lay their eggs under human skin, while black flies bite hard and spread river blindness. As boots and pockets make comfy nests for poisonous spiders, shake out your shoes and zip up your pockets.

## Poison and prey

Steer clear of poison-arrow frogs. The venom on their backs is enough to make you croak. On the plus side, you can dip your arrows in the poison and use them to hunt jungle prey. Watch out that no one is after you, though. Early visitors to Borneo's rainforests fell foul of the fierce Dayak tribes—notorious for beheading and eating the flesh of their enemies. Don't lose your head!

## River dangers

White-water rafting looks fun, but submerged branches can trap you underwater, strong currents can sweep you away, and rapids can smash you to smithereens. If you fall overboard, swim fast! Rivers are home to crushing anacondas, bloodsucking leeches, and electric eels. Avoid any river-based injuries, as blood will attract hungry piranhas your way.

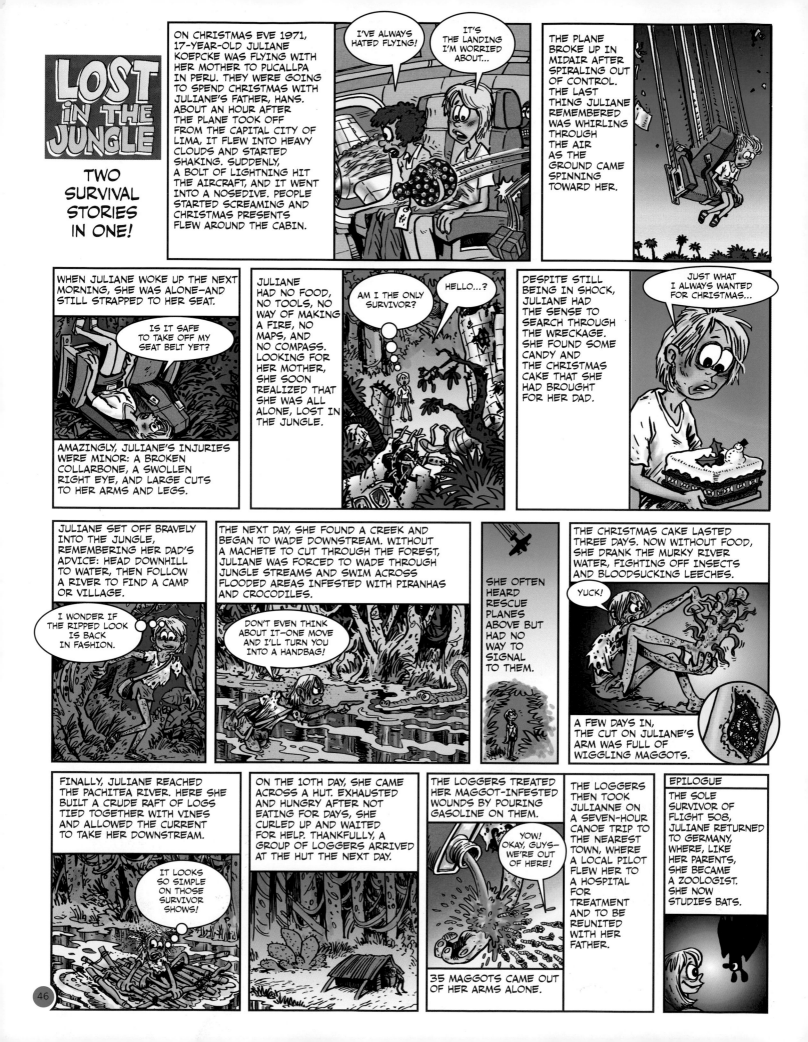

## EQUIPMENT

HARDHAT  ROPE  JACKET  FLASHLIGHT

MAP  BOOTS  FACEMASK  FIRST-AID KIT

# CAVES

The dark, damp, and dangerous world of cave exploring is no place for spelunkers (novice cavers). Spelunker Sam has foolishly entered a deep cave unprepared, unequipped, and on his own. Safely navigate him through the cave maze. Keep your eyes peeled—the cave is handily littered with equipment left by previous potholers.

## LET SLEEPING BEARS LIE

Not so fast! Many large meat-eating animals make their homes in caves, including bears and mountain lions. *Cheat:* Steal that hardhat from below the sleeping bear—it could save Sam's head from falling rocks later on.

## ROCKY HAZARDS

Slipping on rocks, missing jumps, or cracking Sam's head on a stalactite are just some of the rocky hazards to watch out for. *Cheat:* Did you grab that rope? You'll need it to rappel Sam down to the bottom of the cave. Harwood Hole in New Zealand is more than 590 ft (180 m) deep!

## SWEPT AWAY

Hear that dripping? If it's raining outside, a cave can flood very fast. In 2007, eight people drowned in a cave in southern Thailand. When crossing ice-cold underground rivers, watch for dangerous currents. *Cheat:* That waterproof jacket will keep Sam warm and dry.

## GETTING LOST

More people have landed on the Moon than have been inside some of Earth's deepest caves. Get Sam lost in one of these underground mazes and it's "goodbye world"; if he gets stuck for hours in a damp cave, he could catch hypothermia. *Cheat:* Pick up that cave map!

## BAT CAVE

Some caves are home to millions of bats. The ammonia gas released from bat droppings could kill Sam, while inhaling pieces of the cave fungus that grows on them could give him the deadly "cave disease."
*Cheat:* Strap on that facemask.

## DAYLIGHT!

Almost there, but is Sam up for the final climb? Pushing too hard can have deadly consequences; we don't want Sam to be overcome by exhaustion, as it's a long fall down should his muscles weaken and he loses his grip.
*Cheat:* Just take it steady and slow!

## BUG ALERT!

Sam won't meet any monsters, but caves in Borneo are home to giant poisonous centipedes that scuttle across the walls, while creepy cave crickets with antennae as long as your arm live on the sandy cave floor. Ugh!
*Cheat:* Grab that flashlight in case Sam's hardhat light fails.

## CLOSE ENCOUNTERS

Before Sam jumps down the hole, put on those sturdy boots. If you get to a tight spot, be careful that you don't get him stuck.
*Cheat:* Sam doesn't have gloves to protect his hands from razor-sharp rock edges, or kneepads for crawling through tight gaps, so pick up the first-aid kit in case of nasty scrapes.

## TOXIC POOLS

Beware of "foul air." In some caves, the air is laced with poisonous gases such as methane, ammonia, and hydrogen sulfide. Invisible carbon dioxide can lead to clumsiness, dizziness, and death.
*Cheat:* Grab that extra oxygen mask just in case.

## Left for dead

In May 2006, after reaching the summit of Everest the day before but suffering severely from the effects of the altitude, mountaineer Lincoln Hall was left at a height of 28,500 ft (8,700 m) by a rescue party of Sherpas who thought that he was dead. Incredibly, he survived a night near the peak without a hat, gloves, sleeping bag, food, water, or oxygen. He was lucky to escape with no more than severe frostbite.

## A fatal bottleneck

In May 1996, a group of climbers was held up reaching Everest's peak, as some 25 others were attempting the summit on the same day! No one noticed the snow clouds forming, and just two hours later, the climbers were battling against hurricane-force winds and driving snow, leaving five climbers dead.

## Mountain route ▬▬▬

 **BEARS AND COUGARS:** If you feel like a snack, remember that food smells soon get picked up by passing bears and cougars. One in five cougar attacks is fatal, and one swipe from a grizzly paw can take your head off.

 **CREVASSES:** Easy does it. Many climbers have died crossing mountain glaciers after falling into a crevasse—a deep chasm in the ice. A layer of snow can cover the entrance, forming a treacherous snow bridge.

 **FALLING ROCKS:** Don't spend too long admiring the scenery. Rocks can tumble down the mountainside at any moment and knock you loose. Hanging glaciers on steep slopes also drop ice, which hurt. A lot.

 **DISEASES:** Feeling itchy? A bite from a tick could lead to chills, a severe headache, fatigue, deep muscle pain, nausea, and a very nasty rash—all signs of Rocky Mountain spotted fever.

 **AVALANCHES:** Sssshh! Most avalanches are triggered by their victims, so avoid yelling to your fellow climbers or you could get hit by a giant slab of snow and ice streaking down the mountain at speeds of up to 217 mph (350 km/h).

 **FROSTBITE:** Wrap up warm or the frost will bite. Exposed fingers and ears can become black and swollen and, if badly frozen, they will eventually drop off! Climbing is a lot trickier without fingers or toes...

**ALTITUDE SICKNESS:** The views from the top may be wonderful, but don't hang around taking snaps, as the lack of oxygen up here can be fatal, leading to splitting headaches followed by coma and death.

**SNOWBLINDNESS:** Make sure you bring along dark goggles or a pair of sunglasses. They can be a real lifesaver, as gazing at bright white snow for too long can seriously damage your eyes.

 **BLIZZARDS:** A snowstorm can appear from nowhere. Howling winds hurl snow and ice at your body, blasting your face and sucking the heat and air out of you. To top it all, the rest of your party can vanish from sight in the driving snow.

## Exposed summit

Congratulations! You've made it! Now just to get back down again... safely! Time is tight, as you need to get off the exposed peak before night falls and your oxygen tank runs out. Don't dawdle, as the weather here can dramatically change in just a few minutes, and 186-mph (300-km/h) gusts of wind can blow you off the mountain!

## Death zone

Once you climb over 23,000 ft (7,000 m), you enter the death zone. Get stranded here and you'll fall victim to hypoxia—lack of oxygen to the brain. Slowly, you become confused and lose your sense of balance. Soon all you want to do is lie down and do nothing, which is bad news, as it means that you're entering into a coma.

## Determined to survive

In 1985, Joe Simpson injured his knee in a fall when he and Simon Yates were caught in a snowstorm in the Peruvian Andes. Another blizzard struck as Yates was lowering him down the mountain, forcing Yates to cut the rope. Simpson fell 98 ft (30 m) but managed to crawl to camp with just a broken leg.

## Base camp

Even down here you need to keep your wits about you as fatigue takes its toll. Just one slip and you're gone. On the lower slopes of a mountain you'll have to cross glaciers full of dangerous crevasses or risk climbing avalanche-prone mountains of fresh snow that is just waiting to be disturbed...

# MOUNTAIN MADNESS

Day 2. Looking forward to the fresh air and standing on top of the world, but I can't help feeling a little bit nervous, especially after hearing all those tales about the dreaded "death zone"...

## IT'S SNOW JOKE...

When a blizzard hits, all you can do is dig a cave in the ice and hope for the best. In 1982, Mark Inglis and Phil Doole waited 13 days for a storm to pass on top of New Zealand's highest mountain, Aoraki.

## MOUNTAIN SURGERY

Even the lower slopes aren't for wimps. Back in October 1993, Bill Jeracki was fishing up in the Rockies when a boulder rolled onto his leg, pinning him under the rock. In real danger of freezing to death, Bill had no choice but to hack his own leg off with a penknife!

WHOOMPH!

An exploding volcano flings out giant ash clouds that blanket vast areas with a suffocating layer. In 1982, two jumbo jets almost crashed after flying into an ash cloud from Indonesia's Galunggung volcano, while in 2010, Iceland's Eyjafjallajökull volcano turned most of Europe's airspace into a no-fly zone.

# VOLCANO!

Every day, somewhere around the world, 20 volcanoes erupt. Volcanic rock makes up about four fifths of Earth's surface, oozing up through the crust as lava before cooling and hardening. Volcanoes rise up at the boundaries between the "plates" that make up Earth's surface and owing to "hot spots" in Earth's crust. These fiery monsters are fiendishly unpredictable, so expect the unexpected as things heat up...

WHOOSH!

A pyroclastic flow is a flaming cocktail of superhot gas and magma droplets that cascade down the side of a volcano at speeds of up to 435 mph (700 km/h). It can suddenly change direction, with deadly consequences—a flow on Japan's Mount Unzen killed 42 people studying its actions in 1991.

POW!

Sideways volcanic explosions away from the main crater, known as lateral blasts, can fire out seething magma and blocks of rock weighing up to 110 tons (100 tonnes). In 1980, when Mount Saint Helens erupted in Washington State, a blast traveling at more than 620 mph (1,000 km/h) flattened entire forests up to 18 miles (30 km) away.

## ALAKAZAM!

## BANG!

When a volcano erupts, hot molten rock from deep inside Earth bursts out of the ground through an opening in its crust and explodes out of the volcano's main crater. Rocks, ash, mud, and poisonous gases are also flung out. Volcanic eruptions can cause widespread devastation and have killed more than 250,000 people over the past 30 years.

Volcanoes can appear out of nowhere. The cinder-cone volcano Parícutin appeared in a Mexican cornfield on February 20, 1943. Within a week, it was five stories tall, and by the end of the year, it had grown to more than 1,100 ft (336 m) in height.

Heads down! Lumps of glowing lava can cool and harden as they whiz through the air. In 1993, six scientists were killed by one of these "lava bombs" from the Galeras volcano in Colombia. Cowpie bombs are another hazard to avoid—made of fluid magma, they're still liquid when they hit the ground but land with enough thump to flatten you.

## WHAM!

## SIZZLE...

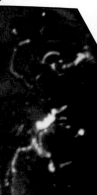

Seething rivers of liquid rock called lava flow down the side of a volcano, burning trees, houses, and anyone unlucky enough to get in the way. Mercifully, most are slow enough for you to dodge, although the rivers of basalt lava that flow from Hawaiian volcanoes can be a speedy 6 mph (10 km/h) and are the hottest known, at a scorching 2,100°F (1,150°C).

## BLASTOMETER

Volcanic eruptions are compared using the volcano explosivity index (VEI), which measures the amount of material released during an eruption. The index ranges from zero (minimal material) to eight (maximum material). The largest known eruption occurred 73,000 years ago in what is now Indonesia—Volcano Toba threw out so much material that it blocked out the sun and plunged the world into an ice age.

---

**8 Megacolossal**
Ejects 240 cu. miles (1,000 cu. km) of material

Occurs every 10,000 years

**7 Supercolossal**
Ejects 24 cu. miles (100 cu. km) of material

Occurs every 1,000 years

**6 Colossal**
Ejects 2.4 cu. miles (10 cu. km) of material

Occurs every 100 years

**5 Paroxysmal**
Ejects 0.24 cu. miles (1 cu. km) of material

Occurs every 100 years

**4 Cataclysmic**
Ejects 0.02 cu. miles (0.1 cu. km) of material

Occurs every 10 years

**3 Severe**
Ejects 353,000,000 cu. ft (10,000,000 cu. m) of material

Occurs yearly

**2 Explosive**
Ejects 35,000,000 cu. ft (1,000,000 cu. m) of material

Occurs weekly

**1 Gentle**
Ejects 353,000 cu. ft (10,000 cu. m) of material

Occurs daily

---

## Side effects

When Earth shakes like crazy, it can lead to all sorts of other deadly disasters. Quakes under the seabed can trigger giant waves, such as the terrifying tsunami that swept across the Indian Ocean in December 2004. They can also set off giant landslides, sending millions of tons (tonnes) of rock and ice crashing down a mountainside. If a quake occurs while people are cooking, like the Tokyo earthquake of 1923, it can set off ferocious firestorms that cause even more damage than the quake itself.

## Ready to rumble

No one can predict earthquakes, but if you're lucky, you may get a warning in the form of tiny tremors, signaling that there's a monster quake on the way. Also, geysers—hot springs that shoot out fountains of water as regular as clockwork—can suddenly go bananas as their water comes from deep underground where the quake begins. Other signs of deep trouble are flashes of blue and red in the sky as underground quartz rocks are shattered into pieces by the shifting rock, creating electric currents that travel up into the air.

## Whose fault is it?

Earth's crust is made up of seven giant, and many smaller, pieces called plates that float around on top of the hot, liquid rock below. As they move around, the plates push and grind against one another in places known as faults. Over time, the pressure builds up, and up… until suddenly the plates jerk past one another, creating an earthquake. Hot spots for this kind of earth-shaking mayhem are California, Japan, and Mexico, while innumerable smaller earthquakes plague parts of Alaska.

## ... and the strongest

The world's strongest recorded earthquake struck Chile in 1960. Measuring 9.5 on the Richter scale, it triggered a 36-ft- (11-m-) high tsunami that swept entire villages up to 1.9 miles (3 km) inland. The surface shock waves were so powerful that they could still be felt two days later. More than 1,650 people were killed and another two million lost their homes.

## The deadliest...

In 1976, the water in a well outside Tangshan, China, rose and fell three times in one day. At 4 A.M. the next morning, the deadliest earthquake in modern times struck the city—most people were still asleep in their beds and had no chance of escape. Measuring 7.5 on the Richter scale, the quake flattened hundreds of thousands of buildings and killed up to 750,000 people.

# AKE, RATTLE, AND ROLL

Earthquakes strike suddenly and without warning. They don't last long, but if you're standing in the middle of one, a minute can seem like an eternity. The ground shakes violently, and buildings, trees, and power lines collapse. In the blink of an eye, whole cities can be reduced to rubble.

## Richter scale

The size of an earthquake can be measured using the Richter scale. Starting from 1, which is the weakest point on the scale, it measures the amount of movement in the ground during a quake, with each point on the scale being 10 times stronger than the one before. At the moment, the biggest earthquake measured 9.5, but there's no limit to how massive future earthquakes could be.

## Wildfires

These forest fires usually start without warning and spread with lightning speed. Air around the fire warms and rises, creating winds that fan the flames, feeding them more oxygen. Giant fires called "gobblers" burn everything in their path, and a sudden shift in the wind can blow the fires in a different direction. The unpredictable nature of forest fires means that people can find themselves trapped unexpectedly, their escape route blocked.

## Historic hot spot

Burning embers from a baker's oven started the infamous Great Fire of London in 1666. This furious fire destroyed 13,200 houses, 87 churches, and Saint Paul's Cathedral, as well as forcing 100,000 people to flee their homes. Thankfully, the loss of human life was minimal. The rats weren't so lucky, though: masses of plague-carrying rats perished in the blaze, happily ridding London of the deadly disease that had ravished it since 1665.

## Seat of the fire

In the U.S. alone, faulty home wiring or unsound appliances cause more than 65,000 fires and kill at least 480 people every year. But any electronic device that is left on with electricity flowing through it has the potential to overheat and burst into flames. In 2007, unlucky American Danny Williams's pants caught on fire when his MP3 player burst into flames in his pocket.

## Watch the gas

Smoke and toxic gases from fires kill more people than burns. The flammable gases given off by burning furniture can suddenly explode—with enough force to blow someone off their feet. Known as a "backdraft," this explosion is caused by oxygen-starved fiery gases being fed air through the opening of a door or window. The particles in clouds of trapped smoke can also ignite, causing a frazzling and frighteningly dangerous ball of flame known as a "flashover."

## Battling the inferno

Firefighters have to cope with blinding flames, choking smoke, and waves of heat. Even when wearing protective clothing, it takes courage to enter a burning building. Walls can suddenly collapse and gas cylinders may explode without warning. It is often so smoky inside that firefighters cannot even see their own feet.

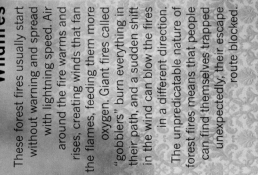

## Heating up

Fires are hot. Even a candle burns at a sizzling 2,200°F (1,200°C). The hottest flames, glowing with a blue hue, are usually at the base of a fire, close to the burning fuel and where there is the most oxygen. The tips of a fire release their heat into the surroundings and so are slightly cooler, flickering orange or yellow.

## Kindling

A fire needs fuel, heat, and oxygen to burn. Cut off any one of these and it goes out. Pouring water or powder onto a fire reduces the heat, while smothering it with a blanket cuts off the oxygen. All fires stop when the fuel runs out.

# WHAT THE BLAZES?

If you play with fire, getting your fingers burned is the least of your worries. A raging fire can destroy your house in under an hour, while out in the open, fire can reduce an entire forest to a pile of ash and charred wood. It's also a deadly weapon; throughout history, fire has been used against enemy castles, ships, and cities. This tempestuous element kills more people every year than any other force of nature.

## Spontaneous human combustion

There are a number of cases of people suddenly bursting into flames, leaving nothing but some smoldering slippers. Some people think it's a supernatural phenomenon; others suggest a scientific reason. One theory is the "wick effect," which claims that a clothed human body is like an inside-out candle—once the clothes catch on fire, the melting human fat provides the fuel to keep burning until there's nothing left but a pile of ash.

# MIGHTY WIND CARNIVAL

Come one, come all! The carnival has blown into town. There's stormy weather ahead, so batten down the hatches. Step right up and feel the power of the mightiest winds: hurricanes, tornadoes, and other deadly windstorms. The stories behind these storms will blow you away.

### HURRICANE

This intense rotating storm is born over warm ocean waters. Bands of tall rain clouds form and grow around a low-pressure system. Wild winds begin to swirl around the calm central zone, called the eye. Hurricanes can be up to 400 miles (650 km) in width, and their destructive winds of up to 200 mph (320 km/h) can rage for days.

### TORNADO

This twisty storm forms in warm, moist air ahead of a cold front. The collision between the high- and low-pressure systems causes the winds to circulate around each other in a tight spiral. The tornado appears as a spinning, funnel-shaped cloud. When the twister touches down on the ground, its winds can fling cars, cows, trees, and people through the air and reduce buildings to rubble.

### WATERSPOUT

A weak type of tornado that forms over water, a waterspout is a spinning column of tiny water droplets stretching from a cloud to the sea. The spout leaves behind bubbles and waves as it zips across the ocean. Waterspouts are hazardous to swimmers, boats, and small aircraft.

**TWISTER**

**TORNADO**

**GOING UP!**

**WILD WATERSPOUT**

KATRINA

### FUJITA SCALE

Tornado winds can spin at 318 mph (512 km/h)—almost half the speed of sound. The Fujita scale is used to measure their destructive power by studying the aftermath of a twister. It runs from F0 (little or no damage to buildings and vegetation) to F5 (everything is as flat as a pancake).

## SQUALL

Sudden and violent windstorms called squalls move across the land in a long line, bringing heavy rain, lightning, and tornadoes. Over water, white squalls blanket the air in a foamy mist, causing a hazard for ships. In the winter, snow squalls create heavy snow and high winds.

## DUST DEVIL

These funnels of dust (also known as dancing devils or whirly-whirlies) form in deserts and other dry places when a sudden rush of hot air rises through cooler air, pulling up a whirlwind of dust. A sight to behold, dust devils can be up to 3,280 ft (1,000 m) in height and 32 ft (10 m) in width.

## HURRICANE NAMES

Hurricane storms are also known as typhoons and tropical cyclones, and each new hurricane is given a name to identify it. The preselected names are in alphabetical order and switch between male and female. The names of very bad storms, such as Katrina, are retired and never used again.

## DERECHO

Named after the Spanish word for "direct," this weird windstorm moves in a straight line, with winds of up to 100 mph (160 km/h) and multiple thunderstorms. A derecho can whip up wild waves over water, tip over cars, and collapse buildings.

# WATERCOLORS

When there's too much water in one place, it can spill over its usual boundaries and cause a flood. Just a brush stroke of bad weather can be enough to paint a different landscape. Heavy rainstorms and melting ice or snow can cause seas, lakes, rivers, and even sewers to overflow. Floodwaters can cause masses of mayhem, wreaking havoc on the land, ruining crops, washing away roads and railroads, and saturating buildings and houses.

## RIVERINE FLOODING

As a river flows toward the ocean, it is fed by both smaller streams and the land draining water into it. Sometimes, owing to heavy rainfall or melting snow, this water runs into the river faster than the river can carry it away, causing it to burst its banks. Such riverine flooding can paint enormous areas of the landscape with its dirty water, while the water's sheer strength can carry cars, trees, and even small buildings away.

## URBAN FLOODING

When a city is pounded with heavy rain, the sewers can quickly reach their full capacity. The excess water overflows the drains and surges out onto the city streets. While urban floods can be a nuisance for pedestrians and drivers, the risk of death or serious damage is low.

## FLASH FLOOD

These unpredictable floods can strike with incredible speed. Flash floods occur when heavy rain hammering down on a small area collects in a gully or stream. The floodwaters move in a strong, rushing current, carrying destructive debris, tearing out trees, and demolishing any structures in their way, from buildings to bridges.

## STORM SURGE

Water that is pushed toward the shore by the force of the winds swirling around a hurricane is called a storm surge.

The advancing surge can combine with the normal advancing tide to create a storm tide. Wind-driven waves on top of this wall of water can pound the coast, weakening structures and drowning the land.

## COASTAL FLOODING

During a severe coastal storm, winds can push the seawater up into huge waves. These batter the shoreline over and over again. The wild waves can eventually rip through sea defenses as the seawater pours inland, flooding coastal areas.

## TSUNAMI

A tsunami is a series of waves traveling across the ocean following an earthquake or volcano erupting on the seabed. When the line of waves approaches the shore, its speed slows, but the height of the water grows. The water along the shoreline recedes at first, exposing areas normally submerged, but when the waves strike land, they can inundate the coastline, wiping out anything in their path.

## Blizzard

This deadly mix of freezing temperatures, howling winds, and heavy snow can cause mass devastation. In January 1888, a "Great White Hurricane" struck the Great Plains of North America, creating snowdrifts about five stories high. Around 400 people died, including children on their way home from school.

# FREAKY WEATHER

Are you bored with sunny spells and outbreaks of drizzle? Fed up with light breezes and a small risk of thunder? But what would happen if the world's freakiest weather came to town? You'll need more than an umbrella if the outlook is frogs tumbling from the sky, skin-sizzling windstorms, and hailstorms as big as basketballs.

## Tornado

The powerful, whirling winds of a tornado will devastate anything that gets in their way. In 1880, a tornado in Missouri picked up a house and dropped it 12 miles (19 km) down the road, while, in 1940, a tornado in Russia picked up an old money chest and deposited coins dating from the 16th century over the town of Gorky. The world's deadliest tornado occurred in 1989, tearing up the land and killing more than 1,300 people in Bangladesh.

## Wild wind

Blisteringly hot windstorms can shrivel everything in their path. When one of these scorchers swept over California in 1850, it killed cows, rabbits, and birds and baked fruit that hung from the trees. In 1991, the diablo winds that blew across northern California led to the most destructive wildfire in U.S. history—about 3,500 homes in Oakland were burned down and 25 people died.

## Colored rain

In the summer of 2001, a downpour of green, red, and yellow rain fell on southern India, staining the clothes of people unable to take cover. At first, people thought that dust from an exploding meteor had caused the colorful shower, but no evidence was found. In the end, scientists tracked down the culprit—algae, growing on local trees, that had released colored spores into the atmosphere.

## Red sprite

This sudden flash of light can sometimes be seen at night above a thunderstorm, about 40 miles (65 km) up in the sky. As well as these ruby-colored lightning streaks, beams of blue can flash across the top of a cloud, known as blue jets and adding to the strange disco-light effect.

## Hailstones

Small pieces of ice can fall during a heavy shower of rain, but hefty hailstones can pose a very serious risk to anyone standing in their path. In 1986, hailstones weighing a whopping 2 lb (1 kg) killed 92 people in Bangladesh. A bizarre incident also occurred in 1930, when four German glider pilots became human hailstones after flying into a storm. They were frozen solid by the time they reached the ground!

## Lightning

A thunderbolt streaks across the sky at speeds of more than 220,000 mph (360,000 km/h), and more than 100 of them strike somewhere on Earth every second. These giant sparks heat up the air around them to a sizzling 48,000°F (27,000°C)—three times the temperature of the Sun's surface. Although lightning strikes can be deadly, American park ranger Roy Sullivan survived an incredible seven strikes during his 36-year career in Virginia.

## Wiggly worms

In 2007, Eleanor Beal was crossing the street in Louisiana when a clump of wiggling worms suddenly dropped from the sky. Animals such as fish, turtles, and frogs have also been known to fall, possibly after being sucked up by waterspouts and then dumped onto land. Amazingly, some animals survive their aerobatic ordeal.

# THE TOTALLY TOXIC TABLE OF POLLUTANTS

Watch out—pollution's about! It's beneath your feet, in lakes and seas, and in the air you breathe. While giant oil spills wreak havoc on wildlife, other pollutants can have deadly consequences for humans. Some may even be causing climate change. In fact, there are so many pollutants that it's difficult to keep track of them all. Whether you see a cloud of something sinister drifting toward you or a horrible green sludge in the water, study up on what's what with this handy table of toxic nasties.

## Radiation

There wouldn't be life on Earth without the constant flow of energy from the Sun. However, radioactive atoms give off rays that destroy plant and animal cells, causing deadly illnesses and horrible mutations. Even scarier, these rays cannot be seen, smelled, or touched. They are also fairly unstoppable—gamma rays can travel through 10 ft (3 m) of concrete!

**Nuclear**

1

**1**. When the Chernobyl nuclear power plant blew up in 1986, 47 people died and another 130,000 people suffered from high doses of radiation. Despite horrible predictions, though, the area is thriving with wildlife today.

**2**. Earth is constantly bombarded by potentially lethal rays from the Sun. Invisible ultraviolet (UV) rays can burn your skin and give you skin cancer.

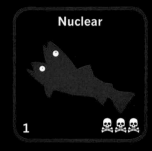

**Solar**

2

## Air pollution

There are all sorts of unpleasant chemicals floating around in the atmosphere as tiny specks of dust, toxic droplets, or invisible gases. Some are caused by volcanic eruptions, burning forests, or rotting plant or animal waste, but many more are created by people.

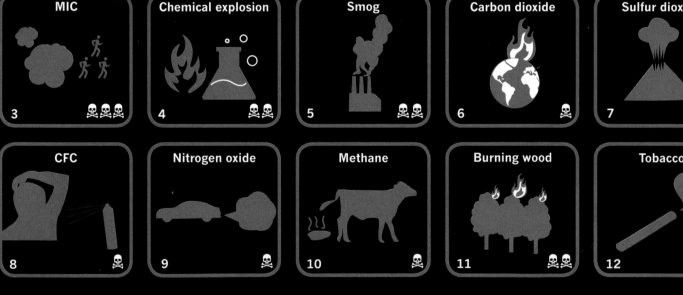

**MIC** 3

**Chemical explosion** 4

**Smog** 5

**Carbon dioxide** 6

**Sulfur dioxide** 7

**CFC** 8

**Nitrogen oxide** 9

**Methane** 10

**Burning wood** 11

**Tobacco** 12

**3**. In 1984 in Bhopal, India, 47 tons (43 tonnes) of methyl isocyanate (MIC) leaked from a factory. The lethal cloud swamped the city, and 25,000 people choked and suffocated.

**4**. In 1976, an explosion at a chemical factory in Meda, Italy, shot toxic gases into the air. The cloud floated downwind and left 193 victims with scarred faces.

**5**. Smog is a mix of smoke and fog. During 1952, more than 12,000 people died in London, England, owing to polluted smog, known locally as a "pea souper."

**6**. The carbon dioxide that spews out of power plants, cars, and factories is a major contributor to global warming, as it traps the Sun's heat in the atmosphere.

**7**. Erupting volcanoes give off clouds of sulfur dioxide. When this gas dissolves in rain clouds, it creates acid rain. This pollutes lakes and rivers and kills wildlife.

**8**. Chlorine in chlorofluorocarbons (CFCs) creates a hole in the ozone layer—a crucial shield from the Sun's harmful UV rays. In 1987, CFCs were banned from many products.

**9**. Gasoline and diesel engines give off nitrogen oxide. This noxious gas destroys the ozone layer, creates acid rain, and causes deadly lung diseases.

**10**. Rotting waste, such as cowpies, release foul-smelling methane, a greenhouse gas that speeds up global warming 20 times faster than the same amount of carbon dioxide.

**11**. Burning forests give off a potent cocktail of carbon dioxide, methane, nitrogen oxide, and methyl bromide (another powerful greenhouse gas).

**12**. Tobacco smoke contains more than 4,000 chemicals. At least 50 cause cancer, and many others such as formaldehyde, arsenic, and cyanide, are poisonous.

## TOXIC RATING

☠ **TOXIC**

☠☠ **VERY TOXIC**

☠☠☠ **DEADLY TOXIC**

## Soil pollution

Toxic chemicals get into the soil in all sorts of ways—from industrial waste, leaky underground storage tanks, and landfill sites to pesticides sprayed on crops. Once in the soil, the chemicals are absorbed by plants, affecting the whole food chain as they move from worms and insects to birds and eventually humans.

**19.** Litter can choke and suffocate many sea animals. Plastics are the worst, as they do not rot or disintegrate. A bottle dropped on a beach can be carried thousands of miles (kilometers) by ocean currents.

**20.** Designed to kill insects, pesticides can also have a devastating effect on other animals. One pesticide, called DDT, almost wiped out bald eagles in the U.S. before its ban in 1972.

**Litter**

**19** ☠

**Pesticide**

**20** ☠☠

## Water pollution

This type of pollution is possibly the world's biggest killer, as about 500 million people around the world do not have access to safe drinking water and have to use contaminated water. Untreated sewage is a breeding ground for deadly diseases, such as cholera and typhoid fever, while factories, mines, and oil wells can all release acids, salts, and other toxic chemicals into rivers, lakes, and oceans.

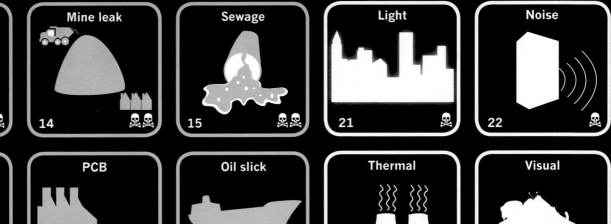

| Mercury | Mine leak | Sewage | Light | Noise |
|---|---|---|---|---|
| **13** ☠☠ | **14** ☠☠ | **15** ☠☠ | **21** ☠ | **22** ☠ |

| Algae bloom | PCB | Oil slick | Thermal | Visual |
|---|---|---|---|---|
| **16** ☠ | **17** ☠☠ | **18** ☠☠ | **23** ☠ | **24** ☠ |

**13.** From 1932 to 1968, 30 tons (27 tonnes) of mercury-laced waste were dumped in the sea near Minamata, Japan. More than 2,000 victims died after eating the poisoned seafood.

**14.** In 1996, about 300,000 truckloads of mining waste leaked from an abandoned mine into two rivers in the Philippines, causing flash floods.

**15.** Raw sewage is a source of dangerous micro-organisms, such as E. coli, and, in 2007, five people drowned when a sewage pool swamped a Palestine village.

**16.** Water pollution can lead to harmful blooms of algae that form "red tides," releasing poisons that enter shellfish (deadly if eaten by humans) and using up all the oxygen in the water, killing fish.

**17.** Polychlorinated biphenyls (PCBs) leaked into rivers from electrical equipment factories and were banned in 1978 after suspicions they caused cancer in those who ate polluted fish.

**18.** When oil spills, it forms a thick black slick that kills large numbers of birds and other sea animals. More than 200,000 sea birds died after the *Exxon Valdez* spill in 1989.

## Sensory pollution

Every day, our senses are bombarded by bright lights, loud noises, and foul smells. A recent report in the Netherlands found that 600 people a year die from stress-related diseases caused by sleepless nights owing to noise pollution. Too much loud music can make you permanently deaf.

**21.** Artificial lights confuse many animals. Turtle hatchlings in Florida rely on moonlight to guide them to water, but bright lights near the beach can make them head in the wrong direction.

**22.** Thanks to machines, we live in a noisy world. At night, the hum of sonar equipment on modern ships is enough to wake residents 15 miles (20 km) from the coast!

**23.** When a power plant first opens, the heat given off by its cooling towers warms up local lakes and rivers so much that it can kill fish and other animals.

**24.** Having to look at billboards, power lines, cell-phone masts, and towering concrete buildings won't kill you, but it does drive some people crazy!

# GLOBAL WARMING

Earth is wrapped in a blanket of gases that trap the Sun's heat like a greenhouse and keep the world at a temperature warm enough to sustain life. Human activity on Earth releases more of these "greenhouse gases," resulting in a thicker blanket and a warmer world. Due to this, our big blue planet is hurtling toward a plethora of big and scary changes that will affect everyone and everything on Earth...

## ❶ STRIKE 1—DROUGHTS

Today, more than 80 million people are affected by droughts owing to high temperatures and little rain. Africa is the worst-affected continent, while Australia has been in the grip of a severe drought for the past decade. The result? Land dries out and cracks, making it unusable for crops, and deserts spread, potentially driving millions of people from their homes—China's capital city, Beijing, is already under attack from giant sandstorms. And due to the heat and dryness, wildfires could become rife, like those that blazed across the U.S. and Australia in 2009.

## ❷ STRIKE 2—STORMS

Since 1980, wild weather has become much more common and has killed 600,000 people. In 2005, 15 hurricanes hit the U.S., including Hurricane Katrina, which devastated New Orleans, while 2007 saw floods in Mexico, India, Bangladesh, and South Korea. Scientists predict more storms, similar to tempestuous Typhoon Tip in 1979, which measured 1,360 miles (2,200 km) across, with winds of 180 mph (300 km/h).

## ❸ STRIKE 3—MELTING ICE

Temperatures are rising twice as fast in the vulnerable Arctic than anywhere else, causing huge sheets of ice to crumble at an alarming rate. The largest single block of ice in the Arctic, the Ward Hunt Ice Shelf, existed for 3,000 years before it started breaking up in the 21st century. The loss of ice is disastrous for polar bears and Inuit hunters, both of whom depend on the ice to hunt seals.

Once the world gets just 3.6°F (2°C) warmer, there may be no going back. The loss of Arctic ice is already replacing reflective white with dark ocean waters that absorb more heat, thereby speeding up global warming.

## ④ STRIKE 4—RISING SEA LEVELS

Due to melting ice at the poles, sea levels could rise by up to 6 ft (2 m) in the next 30 years. This is high enough to swamp the homes of more than 150 million people living in the Nile, Mississippi, and Bengal river deltas. Salt water is already contaminating the underground freshwater supplies of cities such as Shanghai in China, Mumbai in India, and Bangkok in Thailand.

## ⑤ STRIKE 5—ICE AGE

The collapse of the ice sheets could trigger changes in ocean current systems, such as the Gulf Stream in the Atlantic. This warms northern Europe and prevents the bitter winters that are common in places such as Canada and eastern Siberia. If fresh water coming from the melting poles cuts off the Gulf Stream, it could lead to a mini ice age in Europe like that of the 15th and 18th centuries, when the River Thames froze regularly.

## ⑥ STRIKE 6—UNSTEADY EARTH

Melting ice means rising sea levels. Scientists predict that this could trigger volcanic eruptions, earthquakes, tsunamis, and underwater landslides. In 1967, after the Koyna reservoir in India was filled with 8 billion cu. ft (2.5 billion cu. m) of water, the pressure on the ground led to the region's first earthquake, in which 200 people died.

## ⑦ STRIKE 7—ECOSYSTEMS

As Earth keeps warming, many species will struggle to survive in the regions that they now inhabit. For example, many flowering plants cannot bloom without a long period of winter cold to rejuvenate them, and some fish species are already moving north in search of cooler waters. With a predicted rise of 3.6°F (2°C), the warming oceans and increased acidity could kill many of the world's tropical coral reefs.

Way to go, son! Is it just me or is it getting warm in here? I'm feeling a bit bowled over by it all.

# APOCALYPSE NOW!

Since life began here on Earth, life has ended for one species after another through extinction. Typically, a species will become extinct within 10 million years of its first appearance. More than 98 percent of the species that have ever lived are now extinct! When extinction is sudden and catastrophic, it is called a mass-extinction event. What caused these mass extinctions, and what is the forecast for us?

## HOME

### The Big Five

There have been mass extinctions throughout Earth's history, but some were less destructive in terms of biodiversity. The five worst extinctions are known as the Big Five, and each of these events annihilated anywhere from 19 to 90 percent of all species on the planet. Questions about these disasters and their causes remain unanswered. In most cases, the agents of change came from either above (comets or asteroids) or below (massive volcanic activity).

## The Big Five

| Date | Event | Percentage of life lost | Impact | Aftermath |
|---|---|---|---|---|
| 444 million years ago | | 25% | | The **Ordovician-Silurian extinction** was caused by two scenarios occurring one after the other: first there was a drop in sea levels as glaciers formed, followed by rising sea levels as the glaciers melted. Creatures living near the coasts, such as mollusks and eel-like conodonts, were hit hardest. |
| 364 million years ago | | 19% | | No one knows exactly what caused the **Late Devonian extinction**. What we do know is that the temperature dropped massively, twice, perhaps because of ash and dust kicked up by an asteroid collision or volcanoes. Armored fish and primitive reef-forming corals were among the victims. |
| 250 million years ago | | 90% | | The **Permian-Triassic extinction** was the worst by far. The leading theory is that some type of asteroid impact caused this event, but others blame excessive volcanic activity from the Siberian Traps, which spat out enough lava to match the size of Australia. Almost everything both on land and at sea was wiped out. |
| Between 214–199 million years ago | | 50% | | The **End-Triassic extinction** was most likely caused by massive lava floods erupting from the central Atlantic magmatic province—a region covering 7 million sq. miles (11 million sq. km). About one half of the species on Earth, including marine reptiles, were killed. |
| 65 million years ago | | 50% | | The **Cretaceous-Tertiary extinction** (or KT) was probably caused by a huge asteroid that crashed into Mexico, creating a vast crater. The impact triggered fires, earthquakes, landslides, and tsunamis. The debris in the sky would have left Earth in darkness. |

Extinction date to be confirmed

| Cause | Effect |
|---|---|
|  | **Massive asteroid impact**<br>Objects from space crash into the planet all the time, causing varying degrees of damage. If an asteroid the size of a small planet landed on Earth, we would all be wiped out. |
|  | **Huge volcanic eruptions**<br>Imagine the damage caused by a single volcano. In a prolonged eruption of multiple volcanoes, lava would cover the ground and the air would fill with deadly gas and soot. |
|  | **Nuclear war**<br>The odds seem against this now, but a full-scale nuclear war between superpowers would devastate Earth, killing people and blotting out the Sun so that nothing could survive. |
|  | **Black hole**<br>If a black hole approached our solar system, the orbits of the larger planets would change as they were pulled toward it. The Sun and planets would gradually be sucked into the black hole one by one. |
|  | **Expanding Sun**<br>If nothing else happens, Earth will almost certainly come to an end in about five billion years when it falls into the expanding Sun. Forecast: sunny. |

▶ Forecast video

▶ Click to play

▶ MAPS

Earth | Future | GO

## The Sixth Extinction

Scientists estimate that the current rate of extinction is between 100 and 1,000 times faster than the average rate for Earth. We are living in the Holocene extinction event: the Sixth Extinction. During the last century, between 20,000 and two million species have become extinct. But scientists have observed that the rate of extinction is speeding up, linked almost exclusively to

# SPOOKY SPACE

Ready to rev up the rocket ship for a jaw-dropping journey into space? Interested in some prime planetary real estate? Check out the invigorating vapors on Venus or the cool climate of Neptune, then whiz into warp drive and blast through a black hole to a parallel universe. It's a super scary intergalactic adventure!

# ROCKETS AND PARACHUTES

Space travel is a dangerous game, and things can go horribly wrong. The most dangerous times are liftoff—when you rocket up into space—and reentry—when you parachute back down to Earth. Roll the dice and see if you can make it safely from the Launch Pad (square one) back to Mission Control (square 36).

## Rockets: the dangers of liftoff

### 14 No smoking

In the past, rockets used more than 2,200 tons (2,000 tonnes) of fuel just for liftoff. All it took was one spark and… BOOM! In 1960, 91 people were killed when a rocket exploded at a space center in Kazakhstan, then part of the Soviet Union.

### 16 Made of the wrong stuff

In 1967, Apollo 1's command module burst into flames during a run-through, killing the three U.S. astronauts inside. The cause? Possibly a spark created by one of the astronauts' nylon space suits rubbing against a seat.

### 19 One small part, one big explosion

In 1986, just 73 seconds after liftoff, tragedy struck the space shuttle *Challenger*. A small part (the O-ring seal) in the right solid rocket booster failed, allowing hot gases to escape. The gases burned into the shuttle, which broke into pieces and crashed into the ocean, killing all seven crew members.

### 24 Time to bale out

The first four space-shuttle missions in 1981 and 1982 had ejector seats for the commander and pilot but not for the rest of the crew. They worked only going up, as the super-hot temperatures and windblast at supersonic speeds would have killed anyone ejecting during reentry.

### 29 An unlucky strike

In 1969, Apollo 12 was struck by lightning just after liftoff—seriously scary with all that fuel onboard. Luckily, nothing ignited, but since then, if there's a lightning cloud within 11 miles (18 km) of the launch pad, liftoff is delayed. Better safe than sorry.

### 32 No "off" switch

Once a space shuttle's solid rocket boosters are ignited, there's no way to turn them off. They stop only when the fuel runs out. However, on flight STS-68 in 1994, a computer shut down the engine seconds before ignition after sensing a problem.

### 34 Space chimps

Be glad you weren't one of the shrimp, frogs, snails, dogs, or monkeys sent into space—most didn't make it back. The first six monkeys sent up on U.S. rockets were all called Albert, and they all died. Ham the astrochimp (pictured) became the first primate to return to Earth alive.

## Parachutes: the dangers of reentry

### 4 No strings attached

In 1967, the lone occupant of a *Soyuz 1* capsule, Soviet cosmonaut Vladimir Komarov, made it into space and back, only to die when a faulty parachute caused his capsule to slam into the ground at 186 mph (300 km/h).

### 10 Flying a brick

In April 2010, bad weather meant that the landing of flight STS-131 was delayed by two days. When the shuttle finally reentered Earth's atmosphere, the pilot had only one shot at landing as there are no engines to circle around and try again. In fact, the difficult process of gliding and then landing a shuttle is said to be like flying a brick!

### 12 Lucky escape

In 1961, Virgil "Gus" Grissom became the second American to make it into space. Cheers almost turned to tears on his return to Earth when his *Mercury* capsule began to sink after landing in the ocean—a hatch blew open and Grissom almost drowned as water filled his space suit.

### 21 No pressure

Today's astronauts wear pressurized space suits following an accident in 1971: a valve in the *Soyuz 11* capsule became loose during reentry, and the rapid change in air pressure inside killed the three Soviet cosmonauts onboard.

### 25 Delayed disaster

In 2003, during the launch of the space shuttle *Columbia*, a small piece of foam insulation broke loose and hit the left wing at high speed, creating a hole. The intense heat generated during reentry burned into the hole, destroying the wing. The entire spacecraft broke up as it hurtled toward Earth, killing all seven crew members.

# SPACE SURGERY

Hello, this is Hector, your onboard computer. We're currently flying 217 miles (350 km) above Earth. I would say good morning but, given that you'll see dawn another 14 times today as you whiz around the world, why bother? Your three-month health check is due, so please float down to the medical module.

## BODY SCAN IN PROGRESS

### Fitness program

Hector here again. In weightless space, life is effortless, as far as your muscles and bones are concerned. You must maintain fitness levels by working out three times a day. Keep up the good work on the RED (resistive exercise device), but don't pound too hard on the treadmill—it makes the whole station shake! The cycling machine is linked to a heart-rate monitor, so I'll know if you're slacking.

## PATIENT REPORT

1 = low; 5 = medium; 10 = high

### Are you getting enough sleep?

1  2  3  4  5  6  7  8  9  10

**Patient comments**
It's great being able to sleep in any position, and the fireproof sleeping bags are really comfy, but I keep getting woken up! Cosmonaut Ivanov in the bunk next to me snores like a train. Also, my bunk is near the window, and the Sun rises every 90 minutes! I'm having strange dreams, too.

**Hector's notes**
Don't worry, powerful dreams are common among astronauts. If you want to sleep better, I'd recommend an eye mask, which will cut out the bright light from the rising Sun. I'm afraid weightlessness doesn't cure snoring. Maybe try earplugs?

### Do you feel stressed onboard?

1  2  3  4  5  6  7  8  9  10

**Patient comments**
Being cooped up in this tiny capsule is really starting to get on my nerves. I get along okay with most of the crew (even Ivanov the snorer), but Fujita and I almost came to blows the other day when her experiment kept failing and she blamed it on me.

**Hector's notes**
In such a cramped space, be sure to give yourself some "downtime"—listening to music or exercising can really help. Do sort things out with Fujita if you can—on one space shuttle mission, a crew member had to be guarded after he threatened to open the escape hatch!

### Are you eating well?

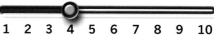

1  2  3  4  5  6  7  8  9  10

**Patient comment**
I'm eating better since I got over my space adaption syndrome, though Symanski got very annoyed when my puke clung to him! I'm slowly getting used to eating in microgravity, but I never feel that hungry, even though there's more than 100 dishes to choose from.

**Hector's notes**
Your body doesn't work as hard in space, so you don't need as many calories as you would on Earth. But make sure your body gets the energy, vitamins, and minerals it needs. Final tip: be careful with crumbly food—breadcrumbs can clog air vents or get into people's eyes, and this is very painful!

## Brain

You've probably noticed that you are feeling a little dizzy and off balance. That's because the receptors in your body got scrambled when you first started living in microgravity. Space adaption syndrome (SAS) will have affected you in lots of other small ways, too—no wonder it's sometimes called "space scurvy." Your brain scan looks fine, but if you feel any symptoms of SAS again, avoid going on any space walks!

## Heart

In space, there's no gravity, so the fluids in your body go in all directions. That's the reason for your puffy face and blocked nose, the cause of your "space sniffles." More seriously, your blood plasma has dropped by 20 percent and your heart has begun to shrink. Regular exercise will cut down the time it takes to recover when you return to Earth.

## Muscles

In orbit, your muscles don't have to fight gravity, so you've already lost 20 percent of your muscle density. Exercise alone won't solve the problem, but hormone pills and gene therapy can help your muscles grow. Be warned: after a 211-day flight on *Salyut 7* in 1983, cosmonauts Anatoli Berezovoy and Valentin Lebedev could barely walk for a week after returning to Earth.

## Bones

After three months, you've lost six percent of your bone density. We can see this from the high calcium levels elsewhere in your body, which can lead to kidney problems. On a two-year mission, your bones could become very weak. You may even lose a few teeth. Taking vitamin D and K pills and undergoing UV light therapy can help in the short term.

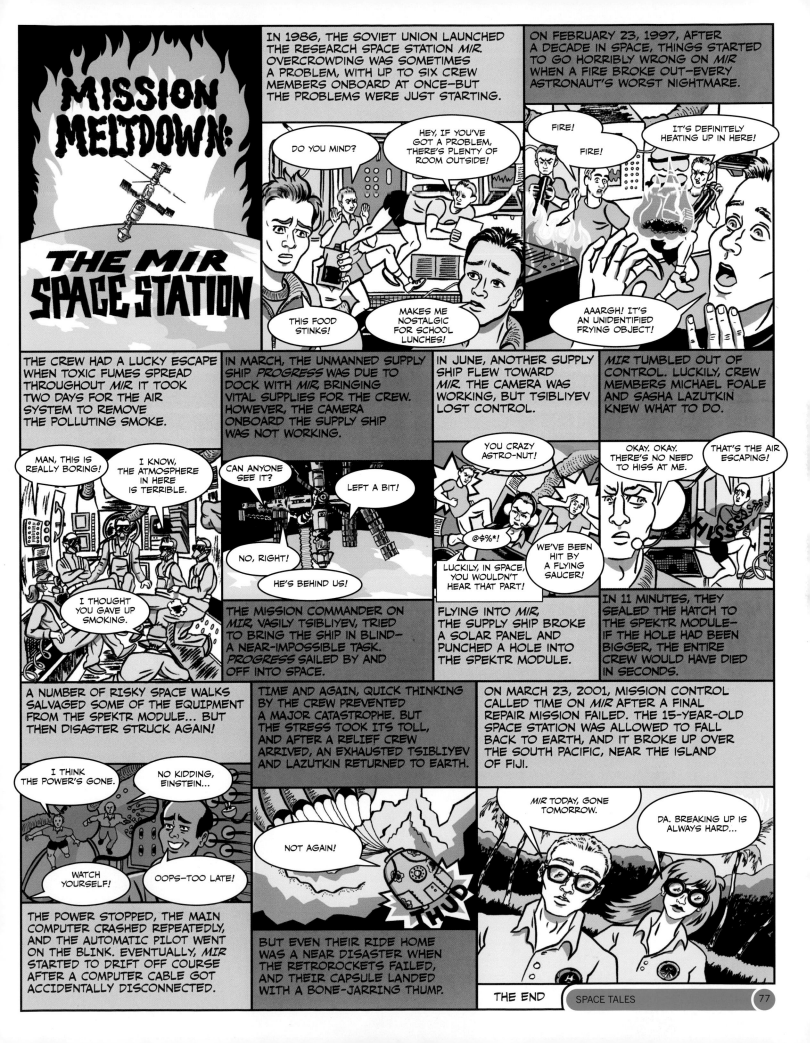

# SPACE ALERT

Space is a dangerous place. If you survive the launch, you must face the perils of Earth's orbit. Maneuver your spacecraft through the hazardous mass of litter orbiting Earth. These pieces of floating debris—or space junk—range in size from tiny flecks of paint to large disused satellites and hurtle through space at a runaway 17,400 mph (28,000 km/h). At this speed, a fragment that is just 0.04 in (1 mm) across has the impact of a bullet. Avoid the space junk to achieve maximum points. Game on!

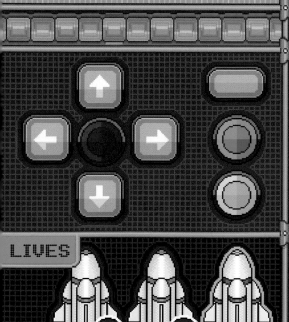

LIVES

**A weighty issue**
There are millions of items orbiting Earth, and more than 13,000 of them are larger than 4 in (10 cm) in diameter. Their combined mass is estimated to be an incredible 5,500 tons (5,000 tonnes!)

**3, 2, 1... blastoff!**
Prepare yourself to be blown away... to space! Strapped to a chair in a tiny metal cabin, on top of a rocket full of explosive chemicals to fire you into orbit, try not to use up all of your lives.

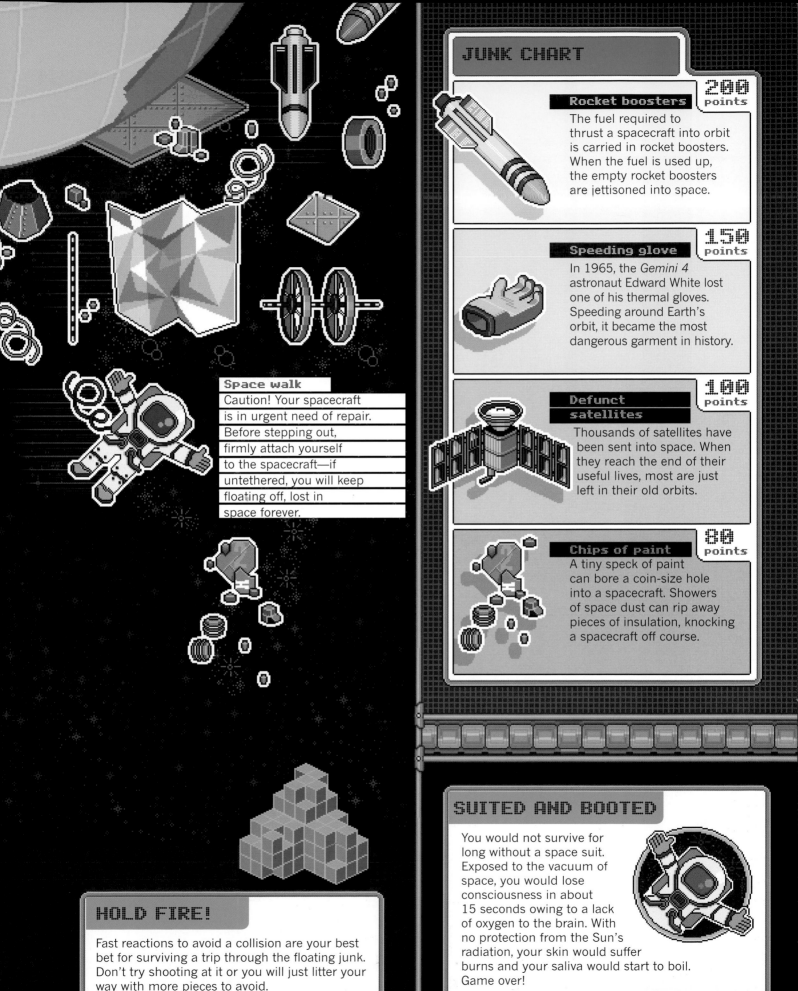

**Space walk**

Caution! Your spacecraft is in urgent need of repair. Before stepping out, firmly attach yourself to the spacecraft—if untethered, you will keep floating off, lost in space forever.

## JUNK CHART

### Rocket boosters — 200 points

The fuel required to thrust a spacecraft into orbit is carried in rocket boosters. When the fuel is used up, the empty rocket boosters are jettisoned into space.

### Speeding glove — 150 points

In 1965, the *Gemini 4* astronaut Edward White lost one of his thermal gloves. Speeding around Earth's orbit, it became the most dangerous garment in history.

### Defunct satellites — 100 points

Thousands of satellites have been sent into space. When they reach the end of their useful lives, most are just left in their old orbits.

### Chips of paint — 80 points

A tiny speck of paint can bore a coin-size hole into a spacecraft. Showers of space dust can rip away pieces of insulation, knocking a spacecraft off course.

## HOLD FIRE!

Fast reactions to avoid a collision are your best bet for surviving a trip through the floating junk. Don't try shooting at it or you will just litter your way with more pieces to avoid.

## SUITED AND BOOTED

You would not survive for long without a space suit. Exposed to the vacuum of space, you would lose consciousness in about 15 seconds owing to a lack of oxygen to the brain. With no protection from the Sun's radiation, your skin would suffer burns and your saliva would start to boil. Game over!

http://www.intergalacticrealestateagents.com

# HOME, SWEET HOME

With all of the space twitter about an imminent asteroid strike on Earth, there's never been a better time to think about buying a second home out in the rugged wilderness of the solar system. Ignore all of those rumors about hostile alien life and make the most of a tranquil setting uninterrupted by annoying pests or noisy neighbors.

**LOCATION** solar system

**I WANT TO** buy

**MIN. PRICE** 300,000 solar dollars

**MAX. PRICE** 500,000 solar dollars

**KEY WORDS** planets, water, life support

Brand new to the market, this gem retains all of its original features. At a refreshing -382°F (-230°C) on the surface, icy Pluto is one of the coldest places in the solar system, so wrap up warm!

## QUOTE OF THE WEEK

*"Thinking ahead, we bought a 1,000-year time-share on Mars and were blown away by the giant sandstorms… The occasional meteor showers are a knockout, too!"* **Jackie Sands**

### MERCURY

**Description:** A scorching surface temperature of 662°F (350°C) during the day and UV rays to die for.
**Conditions:** It has a unique look owing to its highly cratered surface covered with cracked lava.
**Highlights:** Solar wind creates magnetic "tornadoes"—twisted bundles of magnetic fields up to 497 miles (800 km) wide.
**Customer feedback:** Mercury is a similar size to the Moon, so has a familiar feel to it.
**Star rating:** ★★★☆

### VENUS

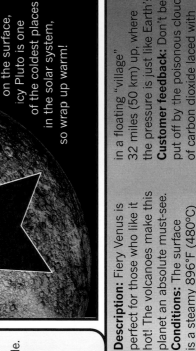

**Description:** Fiery Venus is perfect for those who like it hot! The volcanoes make this planet an absolute must-see.
**Conditions:** The surface is a steamy 896°F (480°C) all year long.
**Highlights:** Avoid the crush on the surface and live in a floating "village" 32 miles (50 km) up, where the pressure is just like Earth's.
**Customer feedback:** Don't be put off by the poisonous clouds of carbon dioxide laced with sulfuric acid—you'll delight in this planet's eerie green light!
**Star rating:** ★★☆

### Victoria Crater: Mars

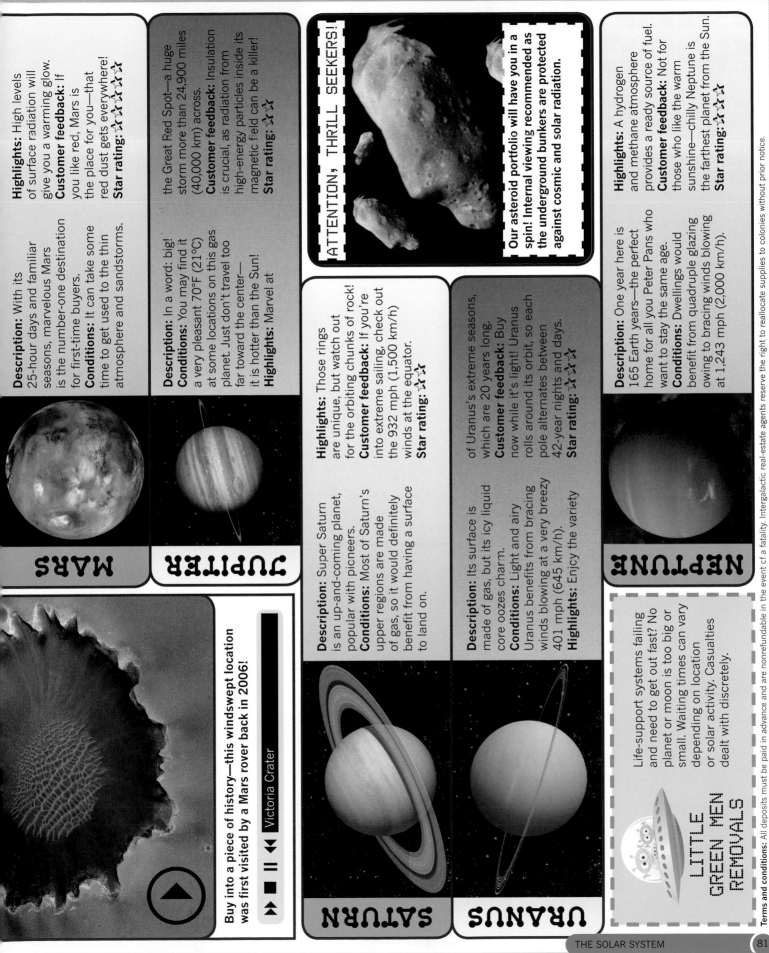

## MARS

**Description:** With its 25-hour days and familiar seasons, marvelous Mars is the number-one destination for first-time buyers.
**Conditions:** It can take some time to get used to the thin atmosphere and sandstorms.
**Highlights:** High levels of surface radiation will give you a warming glow.
**Customer feedback:** If you like red, Mars is the place for you—that red dust gets everywhere!
**Star rating:** ★★★★☆

Buy into a piece of history—this windswept location was first visited by a Mars rover back in 2006!

◀ Victoria Crater

## JUPITER

**Description:** In a word: big!
**Conditions:** You may find it a very pleasant 70°F (21°C) at some locations on this gas planet. Just don't travel too far toward the center—it is hotter than the Sun!
**Highlights:** Marvel at the Great Red Spot—a huge storm more than 24,900 miles (40,000 km) across.
**Customer feedback:** Insulation is crucial, as radiation from high-energy particles inside its magnetic field can be a killer!
**Star rating:** ★★☆

## ATTENTION, THRILL SEEKERS!

**Our asteroid portfolio will have you in a spin! Internal viewing recommended as the underground bunkers are protected against cosmic and solar radiation.**

## NEPTUNE

**Description:** One year here is 165 Earth years—the perfect home for all you Peter Pans who want to stay the same age.
**Conditions:** Dwellings would benefit from quadruple glazing owing to bracing winds blowing at 1,243 mph (2,000 km/h).
**Highlights:** A hydrogen and methane atmosphere provides a ready source of fuel.
**Customer feedback:** Not for those who like the warm sunshine—chilly Neptune is the farthest planet from the Sun.
**Star rating:** ★★★

## SATURN

**Description:** Super Saturn is an up-and-coming planet, popular with pioneers.
**Conditions:** Most of Saturn's upper regions are made of gas, so it would definitely benefit from having a surface to land on.
**Highlights:** Those rings are unique, but watch out for the orbiting chunks of rock!
**Customer feedback:** If you're into extreme sailing, check out the 932 mph (1,500 km/h) winds at the equator.
**Star rating:** ★★☆

## URANUS

**Description:** Its surface is made of gas, but its icy liquid core oozes charm.
**Conditions:** Light and airy Uranus benefits from bracing winds blowing at a very breezy 401 mph (645 km/h).
**Highlights:** Enjoy the variety of Uranus's extreme seasons, which are 20 years long.
**Customer feedback:** Buy now while it's light! Uranus rolls around its orbit, so each pole alternates between 42-year nights and days.
**Star rating:** ★★★

## LITTLE GREEN MEN REMOVALS

Life-support systems failing and need to get out fast? No planet or moon is too big or small. Waiting times can vary depending on location or solar activity. Casualties dealt with discretely.

# PIMP MY SPACESHIP!

How do you revamp an old banger of a space shuttle into a mean, lean light-speed cruising machine? You'll need some serious muscle to reach even our closest star, Proxima Centauri (a distance equal to 50 million trips to the Moon and back). If you want to be a serious cosmic player, you'll also have to deal with nasty bugs, microgravity, radiation, and the risk of a collision. Luxurious features and a bit of bling will keep your crew happy—the last thing you want is a mutiny in deep space!

## Max your comfort

It will be a long ride, so let's rip out those old seats and replace them with comfy chairs and headrests with built-in massage pads. In space, you can play your music as loud as you want, so a thumping audio system is a must.

## Superfly controls

Flying the old space shuttle was like driving a brick with wings, so flip the script with state-of-the-art cockpit controls and an awesome navigation system. Whizzing through space, you'll need these to avoid being splattered by big chunks of space rocks.

Discovery

## Under the hood

Whatever means of propulsion you choose, big power brings big problems. A piece of antimatter the size of a pea could power a spacecraft across the galaxy—or blow it sky-high! Ditto pulse engines, which sling nuclear bombs out the back, creating "phat" shock waves that push the ship forward. Dark-matter engines could use the energy released when dark-matter particles annihilate one another—although no one actually knows what dark matter is made of or how to store it.

## Space jive

Word up! Radio waves travel at the speed of light, but in outer space, you can't talk to anyone on Earth without very long delays. Recorded 3-D holograms of family members and friends will help the crew to retain their sanity while they're cooped up on a long voyage.

## Looking buff

A system of artificial gravity, along with your very own gym suite, will keep your crew in tiptop condition. It is the perfect environment for toning up those wasted muscles after too long floating around in weightless space.

## Keep it clean

Bust this—nasty bugs may lurk inside your spacecraft, and an outbreak could wipe out your crew, so don't skimp when it comes to installing a good filter system. Bringing plants onboard isn't cool, but it will improve the air quality as they soak up pollutants and toxins.

## A well-padded crib

Thick insulation won't big up your space cred, but it will shield you from high-speed particles, which constantly bombard the spacecraft with deadly radiation. Back in the day, aluminum did the job onboard the International Space Station. Tanks of water and liquid hydrogen will be needed for deep space.

## Bling your thing

A large sunroof will let the sunshine in while passing close to solar systems, but in deep space, the darkness could give the entire crew the winter blues. Bright lights combined with a shiny bling finish will cheer them up bigtime.

# DEEP SPACE

You can expect to run into some deep trouble in deep space. Take our galaxy, the Milky Way: it may look like a bunch of harmless stars, but it is really a giant cannibal. Astronomers have detected it ripping apart dwarf galaxies until eventually they are swallowed up by their giant neighbor. In fact, there's a whole tribe of superhero troublemakers out there.

## COLLIDING GALAXIES

Steer clear of colliding galaxies as they slowly pull each other apart, flinging out stars, dust, and gas into long streamers and leaving a trail of castaway stars. As the galaxies collide, they go through each other and then come out the other side in a different shape. However, this galactic tussle can take billions of years, so don't bother hanging around to see who wins!

## SUPERNOVA

Aging stars like to self-destruct in a blaze of glory: imagine an explosion with the force of 20 billion billion billion megatons of TNT. The result is Supernova—a massive burst of radiation brighter than an entire galaxy, a shock wave hurtling through space at 68 million mph (110 million km/h). With such power, she can do serious damage to entire planets. You have been warned.

## SUPERMASSIVE BLACK HOLE

Three billion times the mass of our own Sun, Supermassive Black Hole is gravity gone crazy. Anything that gets too close—gas, stars, and entire solar systems—might be sucked into oblivion. If a planet gets caught in his pull, it would be squashed to the size of a pinhead!

## TWISTER

If you mess with Twister, you mess with his family. This whirling space tornado is some 3 billion miles (5 trillion km) long and is born from extremes of hot and cold inside his mother, Lagoon Nebula. She's an interstellar cloud of gas, dust, and plasma and a nursery for new stars. Plasma blasting out from these baby stars sometimes creates massive stellar jets—shock waves that can travel light-years.

## NEUTRON STAR

Neutron was born during a supernova explosion. Although small—just 10 miles (16 km) across—he's the most dense object in the universe. Don't pick a fight with this heavyweight, as a heaped teaspoon of Neutron-Star material weighs about 110 million tons (100 million tonnes), the same as a mountain!

## DARK MATTER

All of the galaxies, stars, gas, planets, and people combined make up only four percent of the other contents of the universe. So what's the other 96 percent? Lurking in most galaxies is a cloud of invisible "dark matter," while mysterious "dark galaxies" roam undetected in space. Luckily, they don't seem to react with ordinary matter—but what so they'll leave you alone can unleash, powers this dark one knows for sure.

# TIME TRAVEL

Traveling through time may seem like science fiction, but some scientists think that there are some serious science facts in the idea: from Einstein, whose theory of relativity shows that time is not fixed, to quantum physicists, whose study of subatomic particles point to the possibility of parallel worlds. So, with a little help from a cosmic string or a wiggly wormhole, will we be boldy going where no others have gone before? Only time will tell.

## COSMIC STRINGS

Grab onto a cosmic string and use its immense gravitational pull to travel at incredible speeds. These stringlike objects were probably formed in the early stages of the universe, and may line the entire universe. Their gravitational force is so strong that it could bend space and time to allow time travel.

## TIPLER CYLINDER

American astronomer Frank Tipler's idea for a time machine involves taking a dense chunk of matter and rolling it into an infinitely long, fast-spinning cylinder. If a spaceship followed the right spiral course around the cylinder, it could emerge thousands of years from its starting point. Of course, building an infinitely long cylinder would be quite a challenge!

LOOKS LIKE YOU'VE GOT THE BUBONIC PLAGUE.

HUNTING DINOSAURS WAS GREAT. I SHOT ONE THAT HAD WINGS LIKE A BIRD.

WHAT'S A BIRD?

QUARANTINE

## ARRIVALS: PAST

UP TO DEPARTURES

## PLAGUE CARRIERS

Diseases and infections are endlessly mutating or changing, so a vaccine that protects you against typhoid fever today wouldn't necessarily work if you traveled back to Roman times. There's also a strong chance that you would carry nasty bugs back with you that could wipe out your ancestors.

## GOODBYE, HUMANS

Over millions of years, shrewlike creatures living at the time of the dinosaurs evolved into mammals and eventually into humans. Now imagine what would happen if some clumsy oaf traveled back in time and obliterated our furry ancestors. You've guessed it—no shrews, no humans.

## FASTER THAN THE SPEED OF LIGHT

Einstein's theory of relativity shows that time slows as an object nears light speed—more than 671 million mph (1 billion km/h). Anyone traveling in space close to the speed of light would age less than those left behind on Earth. So traveling faster than light speed could, in theory, allow time travel.

## GRANDFATHER PARADOX

If you went back in time and accidentally killed your grandfather before your father was born, you couldn't exist. Some scientists say that nature would stop this paradox, while others think that the event would create parallel worlds, so Grandpa would live on in the world "next door."

*GRANDFATHER! IS THAT YOU? BUT I ACCIDENTLY RAN YOU OVER IN 1946!*

## DEPARTURES: TERMINAL 1

## BLACK HOLES

Wannabe time travelers could also jump through a rotating black hole. This would then carry them along a wormhole to an exit point, or "white hole," at another point in time. However, travelers would need to zip through to the other side faster than the speed of light so that they are not crushed by the black hole. Oh, and after all that, the travelers must find a safe way back!

## DISAPPEARING ACT

All this talk about time travel could make anyone giddy with excitement. Why would people wait for the future to arrive one day at a time when they can get there anytime they want? And, if the future turns out to be so amazing, why would they ever want to return to the here and now? This one-way ticket could mean a disappearing population problem for the present.

## ARRIVALS: FUTURE

## BLASTS FROM THE FUTURE

Ever fantasized about what the future might hold? Perhaps we finally meet aliens and vacation on Venus. But, if time travel is possible, what if criminals go back in time to blast us with high-tech weapons that we can't defend ourselves against? It hasn't happened yet, so hopefully any time travelers will simply be well-wishers with information about amazing new medicines and how to solve global warming!

*IT RAINS DONUTS IN THE FUTURE!*

*WHAT ARE WE WAITING FOR?!*

*ARRRRRGH!*

# TRUE ALIENS?

Could life exist elsewhere in the universe? In 1961, American astronomer Frank Drake formulated an equation that suggested there were 10,000 alien civilizations that we could potentially communicate with in the Milky Way galaxy alone. Today, scientists have sent satellites into space and set up huge radio telescopes on Earth in search of extraterrestrial beings. But have they already made contact? Study these stories of human encounters with alien beings on Earth... do *you* believe?

## Travis Walton abduction

In 1975, in Arizona, Walton and his fellow loggers were driving home when they saw a glowing object on the roadside. Investigating it, Walton felt as if he'd been hit by a thunderbolt. He awoke, frozen in pain, lying on a table inside a spacecraft. Three aliens were probing his body with medical instruments. Search teams could not find Walton, but he reappeared five days later.

## Australian alien

Driving home in Melbourne, Australia, in 1972, Maureen Purdy was amazed to see a flying saucer hovering in the sky. Two weeks later, she saw it again. This time, her car stopped dead and she heard an otherworldly voice. Months later, the voice told her to come to a meeting place. She took along a witness... Purdy went into a trance and said that an alien wearing a gold foil suit was sitting next to her, but her companion saw and heard nothing.

## Alien abduction

In 1961, American couple Barney and Betty Hill drove along a U.S. highway. Puzzled by an odd light in the sky, they left their car to investigate but could recall nothing else until they arrived home. Under hypnosis, both told the same story: they had been abducted by aliens with gigantic eyes who gave them painful medical examinations.

## Men in Black

Alien encounters are bizarre, but wait until you hear what may happen next: the arrival of the Men in Black (MIB). These shadowy figures have been known to visit UFO spotters, seemingly to suppress information. In 1953, three MIBs visited American UFO buff Albert K. Bender and ordered him to stop his research. Bender reported that his strange visitors were not human, but others on the receiving end of MIB visits believe that they are CIA agents in disguise.

## Aliens on the beach

On a beach in Spain in 1989, a horrified group of teenagers gasped as a pair of alien figures turned into "humans." The male and female creatures walked along the beach and vanished into a crowd, while a UFO hovered in the sky above. The creatures returned and were captured on camera by the teenagers. A trail of footprints left by the aliens led into the sea.

## Moor mystery

In 1987, Philip Spencer was walking in the Ilkey Moor in Yorkshire, England, when he spotted a small alien. He snapped its photo and then ran after the creature, following it to a domed craft that shot up into the sky. He discovered that the compass in his pocket had become reversed, as it was exposed to an extreme amount of energy.

## Crash landing

In 1989, Russian military police who were investigating reports of a UFO found a cigar-shaped ship crashed on the ground. Inside the craft were three blue-green aliens, two dead and one dying. Their hairless skin resembled a reptile's, their fingers were webbed, and they had huge black eyes. Their bodies were reportedly taken to a top-secret military base.

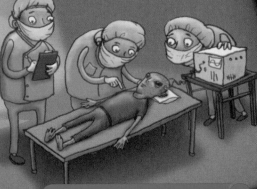

# SCARY SCIENCE

Investigate the fearsome forces of science, from beastly biohazards and bone-cracking crash tests to nuclear meltdowns and mind-bending math. Meet the screwball scientists who experimented on themselves, and come face to face with the freaky creatures created in the name of research. Tread carefully—it's explosive stuff!

# MAD SCIENTISTS

Throughout history, many important advances in science and medicine were the result of people experimenting on themselves. Whether they were doctors who had a taste of their own medicine or scientists who were willing to be the experiment, these radical researchers pushed the limits to test their theories. Were they crazy in a good way or just crazy? Let them tell their stories, and then you can decide.

## Barry Marshall

Everyone said that stress causes stomach ulcers, but I thought the culprit might be a common bacterium, *Helicobacter pylori*. So I downed a petri dish full of the stuff, and, sure enough, a few days later, I came down with gastritis. A course of antibiotics soon put things right. And here's something to raise a glass to: I won a Nobel Prize in 2005. Cheers!

## Alexander von Humboldt

As a great naturalist, botanist, zoologist, and artist of the early 19th century, I practically invented multitasking. I had a theory that mechanical and chemical forces worked together to sustain life. While researching whether the human body had electrical currents, I held an electric eel in one hand and metal in the other to make the charge that went through me stronger. Shocking!

## John Scott Haldane

Breathing in deadly fumes while locked inside a sealed chamber? It's a gas! I researched the effects of different gases in 1927 by sniffing them to see what happened to me. It caused quite a stink, although the results were nothing to sniff at—I developed a gas mask and figured out how deep-sea divers could avoid getting "the bends" (decompression sickness).

## Sir James Young Simpson

Humboldt, you clearly were a man in charge. As a doctor in the 1800s, I knew medical procedures were a pain, so I wanted a good anesthetic. One night at my place, a few friends and I tried inhaling chloroform. We woke up the next day under a table! I'd found a safe way to put patients (and friends) to sleep. How's this for a royal request? In 1853, Queen Victoria used chloroform for a pain-free birth.

## Santorino Santonio

These guys are lightweights! Every single day, for 30 years, I weighed myself, as well as everything I ate and drank and everything I released in the toilet. I noticed a gap between the weight of what went in and what came out. I deduced that the human body is continually losing fluid—a major development in medicine by any measure. Pah!

## Dr. Werner Forssmann

Let's have a heart-to-heart. While working as a hospital intern in 1929, I slid a thin tube called a catheter into a vein in my elbow all the way up to touch my beating heart—something it was forbidden to do. I got an amazing x-ray picture for proof. I also got fired. Researchers later developed cardiac catheterization for heart surgery.

## Kevin Warwick

A heart-warming tale, Forssmann. My turn now. I have a microchip embedded in the nerves of my left arm. Yes, I'm a cyborg, working on connecting my nervous system to the Internet. My research may help doctors to find new ways to treat nervous-system disorders, although the idea of putting microchips in humans makes some scientists a little… nervous.

## Anthrax on Gruinard

*Department of War, 1942*

Research scientists are testing the possibility of using the deadly bacterial disease anthrax in germ warfare against Germany. Bombs containing anthrax spores have been exploded on the remote Scottish island of Gruinard. Spores were breathed in by the island's sheep, and they died within days, proving the highly fatal nature of the bacteria. The island is likely to remain contaminated by spores and be uninhabitable for many years.

TOP SECRET

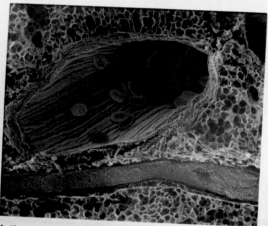

Update: 1990
Gruinard is
now free of
anthrax spores.

Anthrax spores (purple) inside an air passage (blue) within the lung.

A mushroom cloud, created by the first test explosion of an atom bomb that took place in New Mexico on July 16, 1945.

## Memo: Manhattan Project

*Site Y, 1945*

I can finally tell you what has been happening here since the start of World War II. We've been based in Los Alamos, New Mexico, and from 1942 onward, we scientists, gathered from all over the U.S., have been working in top-secret conditions. Our sole task is to develop an atom bomb—a highly advanced weapon that releases the energy inside atoms with truly devastating effects... In August it is going to be dropped on Japan to persuade them to stop fighting.

This is for your eyes only. Do NOT mention my name.

# TOP SECRET

Hidden from public view and away from the prying eyes of rivals, secret laboratories have been carrying out experiments for years. From developing more powerful weapons to discovering untraceable ways of removing troublesome citizens, these national secrets have always been clouded in mystery... until now.

## Poison legacy

*London, September 11, 1978*

The recent assassination of dissident Bulgarian writer Georgi Markov (right) used a method developed in Soviet Russia. Between 1939 and 1953, a team led by secret service head Lavrenti Beria devised ways to kill enemies without leaving any traces. These included an umbrella tipped with a pellet containing the deadly poison ricin. The Bulgarian secret service used this to kill Markov. He was jabbed on Waterloo Bridge here in London, England, four days ago and died today.

### CONFIDENTIAL

### CONFIDENTIAL

### Poison pen

Chechnya, 2002
Reports suggest that Lavrenti Beria's murderous legacy still continues, even though the communist era is over. It is alleged that Omar ibn al-Khattab, rebel leader of the breakaway former Soviet Republic of Chechnya, has been assassinated by the FSB, the Russian secret service. A letter written in poison pen was delivered to Khattab, who died shortly after opening it.

### CLASSIFIED

### FOR YOUR EYES ONLY

.... / .... / ....

## Area 51

*Nevada, 2010*
I'm hurriedly writing to you from just outside the perimeter fence of this top-secret U.S. air base; the security guards are descending on me to move me on. It is generally agreed that new aircraft are tested here, but I'm still suspicious and think this is just a cover. Their failure to offer a better explanation than "it was a weather balloon" that crashed in Roswell in 1947 is strange. I, along with others, think it was alien spacecraft and believe this photo to be proof. What do you think? Are they telling the truth or is it a conspiracy?

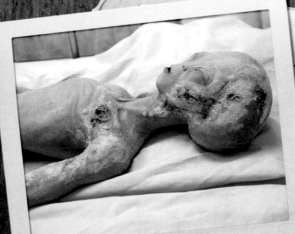

Official sources say that this photograph is a fake, but some people insist that this is a badly injured alien, recovered after the Roswell incident.

# IN THE NAME OF SCIENCE

Scientists routinely carry out experiments to see if their theories are correct or not. But some scientists have taken this to the extreme. Today, for only one day, we've put on view eight of the oddest, freakiest, and downright scariest experiments conducted in the name of science.

## Back from the dead

Bringing the dead back to life was the goal of American researcher Robert Cornish. In 1934, he revived a dead dog named Lazarus using drugs and a type of seesaw to get the blood circulating. But when he asked to try the technique on a death-row prisoner, he found he was barking up the wrong tree.

## Web designers

Spiders instinctively weave perfect webs to catch insects. In 1948, German scientist Peter Witt discovered that giving drugs to spiders made them weave abnormal webs. He then spent a lifetime showing how different drugs altered a spider's web design.

## Expressions and decapitations

In 1924, American psychologist Carney Landis wanted to discover if emotions such as disgust, shock, and joy produced the same facial expressions in different people. He photographed volunteers as they were exposed to various experiences, including asking them to decapitate a live rat!

DOG TREATS

## Stargate project

Could clairvoyants spy on foreign governments over long distances? That's what the Central Intelligence Agency (CIA) in the U.S. wanted to find out. With no useful information after 25 years, the $20-million Stargate project was terminated in 1995.

## Long rest

How do you test what happens to the body during a long space journey without actually going into space? In 1986, researchers in Moscow, Russia, simulated the weightless conditions of space by keeping 11 male volunteers lying on their backs for 370 days. Despite exercising on their backs, the results showed shrunken muscles, lighter bones, and terrible boredom and stress.

## Black vomit

In 1804, American doctor Stubbins Ffirth performed some revolting experiments to test his idea that deadly yellow fever was not infectious. He drank bloody black vomit from a fever patient and rubbed it into his eyes. He didn't get infected, so he considered his case proven. We now know that the disease is spread by mosquitoes.

## Real or robotic?

In 2003, researchers decided to find out if real dogs would accept a robotic dog as if it were a living puppy. Although the dogs sniffed and growled at the dogbot, their reaction was much weaker than with a real dog.

## Obedience to authority

In 1963, American psychologist Stanley Milgram tested the idea that people would carry out atrocities if ordered to by an authority figure. An astonishing 65 percent of participants gave what they thought were lethal electric shocks to an unseen victim in another room.

## Recipe for disaster

Sometime in the 9th century, the Chinese found the recipe for gunpowder. They mixed fuel (carbon-rich charcoal) with a stabilizer (sulfur) to keep things under control and an oxidizer (nitrate) to feed the chemical reaction. When ignited, it went boom!

## KABOOOOOM!

An explosive is a substance packed with stored energy that is released as a sudden blast of expanding gas, bright light, and searing heat. There are two basic types of explosives: low explosives like gunpowder expand slowly, making them useful as propellants (such as to fire a bullet from a gun), while high explosives expand in an instant, creating a destructive shock wave. Enjoy this mind-blowing trip through the archives of explosive history.

## Blasted ants!

The charcoal for gunpowder making came from burned trees, the sulfur from underground mines... but collecting the final ingredient, potassium nitrate, was a stinker of a job: old animal droppings were left to turn white, and then the crystals of nitrate were rinsed off. Gunpowder may initially have been used as an early insect repellent to smoke out invading ants, but, before long, its potential as a weapon was being fully exploited.

## Safety fuse

In the 10th century, the Chinese developed a fuse to delay the ignition of gunpowder. An English leather tanner named William Bickford went one better and invented the modern safety fuse in 1831. After watching a friend make rope, he wrapped a core of gunpowder inside a twist of string and, voilà!—the modern fuse was born, enabling miners to set off explosives from a safe distance. Phews all around.

## Dynamite discovery

Italian chemist Ascanio Sobrero discovered the highly unstable liquid explosive nitroglycerin in 1847. Then, in the 1860s, Swedish entrepreneur Alfred Nobel mixed the more stable solid nitroglycerin with sodium carbonate and a shock-absorbing powder to make dynamite. The creator of this weapon of mass destruction gave his name to the Nobel Peace Prize.

## Dams to diamonds

Dynamite, usually sold in paper-wrapped sticks, was a smash hit in industry. It was used to mine important materials such as steel, copper, silver, and gold, and the transportation system, from roads to tunnels, was built by blasting away rock with dynamite. Other large-scale construction projects, from dams to canals, also relied on its useful obliterating capabilities, as well as the precious South African diamond mines.

## TNT

In 1863, German scientist Joseph Wilbrand discovered TNT (trinitrotoluene)—a yellow chemical explosive that is more stable than dynamite. TNT can be melted down and poured into shell casings, making it valuable in weapon making, although its yellowness rubs off on anyone who handles it; workers who used TNT in World War I weapon factories were nicknamed "canaries," as the chemical turned their skin bright yellow.

# BIOHAZARD GALLERY

Welcome to our Biohazard Gallery. Feel free to wander around and examine the world's nastiest biological hazards—the bacteria and viruses that cause diseases. These are split into four levels, depending on how dangerous they are. On show today are levels 3 (to the left) and 4 (to the right). These are especially perilous, so it is important that you don your protective hazmat suit first.

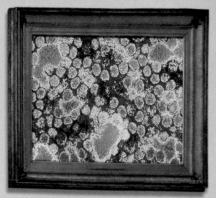

## YELLOW FEVER

This is a clear view of the virus (green) that causes yellow fever in hotter parts of Africa and South America. Spread by bloodsucking mosquitoes, yellow fever produces sweating and nausea and, in serious cases, liver damage and internal bleeding. Fortunately, there is a vaccine against the disease.

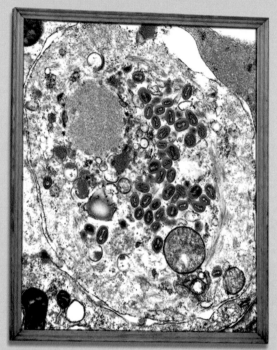

## TUBERCULOSIS

The first exhibit shows the bacteria that cause tuberculosis (TB)—once a killer before the use of antibiotics. These bacteria pass from person to person when someone infected sneezes, coughs, or spits. TB mostly affects the lungs, causing constant coughing, sweating, weight loss, and eventually death. Worryingly, this disease is on the rise again.

## SMALLPOX

Here is a rare chance to see a virus (red) that has been eradicated throughout the world by the use of vaccines. Samples of the virus are kept for research in a few laboratories. In earlier times, smallpox was a devastating and deadly disease that caused severe blistering and scarring.

## WEST NILE VIRUS

Take a look at a virus that's on the move. Once confined to Africa, the West Nile virus has spread across the U.S. since 1999. It is passed on by mosquitoes that bite infected birds and then bite people. Most victims get a headache and a high temperature, but a few suffer from inflammation of the brain, too.

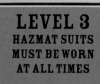

LEVEL 3
HAZMAT SUITS
MUST BE WORN
AT ALL TIMES

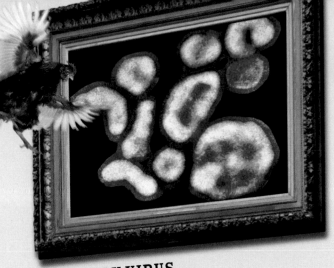

## DENGUE

Level 4 introduces another exhibit featuring a tropical disease. Found in more than 100 countries, dengue hemorrhagic fever is caused by a virus (yellow) that is spread by mosquitoes that feed on blood during the day. Once infected, a person develops headaches, plus muscle and joint pains, before going into shock.

## AVIAN FLU VIRUS

A virus that gives birds the flu might seem like an odd inclusion in the Biohazard Gallery. However, the avian flu virus can sometimes cause a nasty, often fatal, type of flu in humans. There is also a risk that it might become more infectious to humans, who tend to pick it up from handling infected poultry, and spread around the world.

## MARBURG VIRUS

The deadliest exhibit in the Level 4 collection takes its name from the German town of Marburg. It was here, in 1967, that laboratory workers picked up the deadly virus from African monkeys. Spread by infected blood, feces, saliva, or vomit, the Marburg virus causes severe internal bleeding and often death.

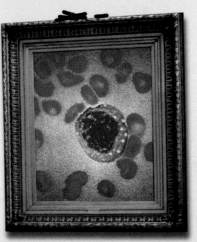

## HANTAVIRUS

This exhibit has a close association with rodents. Those unfortunate enough to pick up the hantavirus usually do so by breathing in particles from the dried droppings of infected mice. The virus makes blood vessels in the lungs very leaky, causing severe breathing problems that can lead to death.

## LEVEL 4
### NO ANIMALS ALLOWED IN THE GALLERY

## HAZMAT SUITS

You may find it uncomfortable to wear, but your hazmat (hazardous materials) suit will provide total protection. Equipped with its own air supply and two-way radio, it encloses your body and is sealed to keep out biohazards.

Come inside and take a look around. I'm Frankenstein's very own monster, a human-crafted creation. In that sense, I'm similar to all of these strange pets that have arrived today, fresh from our laboratories. Some were specially bred, while others were made by altering their genes, and Earmouse was just thrown together! They may look a little bizarre, but have a heart. They do deserve good homes after all they've done for scientific research.

## Milky goodness

This goat seems perfectly normal, but her milk is out of the ordinary. Genetic modification of goats is producing changes in their milk that will be useful to humans. For example, using spider genes, scientists have produced goats that release spider-web proteins in their milk. These are used to make ultrastrong "biosteel" fibers, used in medicine and industry.

**OPEN**

## Earmouse

This isn't a mouse with super hearing. "Earmouse" was developed to see if human organs could be grown in the laboratory. Scientists made an ear-shaped scaffold that they "seeded" with human cartilage cells and joined to the mouse so that its blood supply would nurture the new organ.

## Self-shearing sheep

It may look a bit shabby, but this self-shearing sheep could be the sheep of the future. Instead of having its winter coat cut in the spring by sheep shearers, this new breed automatically sheds its wool. Good news for farmers! It's the result of breeding native ewes (females) with self-shearing rams (males).

# STORE

## Cama

This is a cama—a cross between a camel (from Africa and Asia) and a llama (from South America). Living so far apart, these related animals would not normally breed. However, scientists in Dubai, U.A.E., combined camel sperm with llama eggs to create the cama in the hope that it will produce more wool and meat than regular llamas. Do you have room for him at home?

## Cloned dogs

If your pet dog is getting old, why not replace it with an identical but younger clone? Scientists can now take cells and create an embryo that is implanted inside a surrogate mother. With luck, nine weeks later, out pops a puppy identical to your precious pooch. Cloned breeds so far include Labradors and Afghan hounds.

## Giant salmon

Even if you really like salmon, would you eat one that grows twice as fast, and is seven times as big, as a regular salmon? Scientists have introduced a gene into farmed salmon that greatly increases the production of a growth hormone. These bigger, faster-growing salmon make more money for farmers.

## Sphynx cat

All cat breeds were produced by mating cats with features that breeders wanted to reproduce. The most obvious feature of the Sphynx cat is a lack of fur. This came from a mutation (mistake) in one of the genes. Breeding mutant cats has created the Sphynx breed.

## Glowing mice

There's no problem finding these mice in the dark. Shine an ultraviolet light on them and they glow bright green. Glowing mice are transgenic—they've had a gene inserted into them from another organism, in this case a fluorescent jellyfish. A huge advance in genetics.

# RADIOACTIVE!

Everything we know about radiation has been discovered only in the past 100 years or so. In large doses, it is one of the most dangerous discoveries ever known, but, through trial and error, we've figured out that small doses of radiation can be utilized for positive, sometimes life-saving, effects.

## What is radioactivity?

Most atoms have stable nuclei—the number of neutrons and protons in the nucleus stays the same. But others, such as uranium atoms, have unequal numbers of neutrons and protons. This makes them unstable and liable to break down. When an unstable atom decays (breaks down), it releases particles from its nucleus. This release is called radioactivity.

Particle released from the nucleus

Nucleus

Thick paper

Thin copper

Thick lead

Alpha radiation

Beta radiation

Gamma radiation

## Powerful particles

There are three main types of radiation: alpha, beta, and gamma. Alpha radiation is the weakest type, struggling to pass through a thick sheet of paper. Beta radiation is stronger but meets its match in a thin sheet of copper. Only a thick sheet of lead or concrete can block the most penetrating type of radiation, high-energy gamma rays.

## Discovering radioactivity

French scientist Antoine Henri Becquerel discovered radioactivity by accident in 1896 when he found that uranium salts emitted rays capable of penetrating black paper. Working in Becquerel's lab, Marie Curie and her husband, Pierre, duplicated his experiment in 1897 and named the phenomenon "radioactivity." The Curies devoted their lives to understanding radioactivity, and in 1903, all three scientists shared the Nobel Prize for physics.

## Glowing with health?

In the early 20th century, people weren't aware that exposure to radiation damages human tissue and causes genes to mutate. Tiny amounts of radioactive materials, especially radium, were added to all kinds of products in the belief that they could provide a miracle cure for any ailment. Radioactive drinking water, toothpaste, face cream, bath salts, and medicines all lined pharmacists' shelves.

*Burkbraun*
RADIUM
SCHOKOLADE
RADIUM

*Doramad*

## Eben Byers

The case of Eben Byers (1880–1932) spelled the end of the craze for radioactive products. An American businessman and enthusiastic golfer, he was advised by his doctor to drink radium-laced water to help with an arm injury. After a few months of downing two or three bottles a day, radium had accumulated in his bones and holes had begun to form in his skull. In only two years, he was dead, buried in a lead-lined coffin to avoid contaminating the graveyard soil.

## Everyday exposure

In the modern world, we come into contact with small amounts of radioactive materials every day. If you live near a power plant, have ever traveled by jet, worn a glow-in-the-dark watch, or had an x-ray, you've been exposed to radiation. But now that we understand what a safe amount of radiation is, there's no need to worry about ending up like Eben Byers.

## Put to good use

Today, key cancer drugs are made from radioactive materials, and ingesting small radioactive particles and following their path through the body is an important medical diagnostic tool. Airline security x-rays that protect us in the skies by detecting weapons of terror, and smoke detectors that keep us safe at home, also use small amounts of radioactive matter.

# THE MOST DANGEROUS EQUATION

December 31, 1905

Dear diary,

What a miraculous year it has been for me, Albert Einstein. The ideas that have been tumbling around in my head have finally come together. Now, I have the first draft of my equation...

Energy $\longrightarrow$

$$E = mc^2$$

Speed of light, squared (i.e., the speed of light multiplied by the speed of light)

Mass (i.e., the quantity of matter in any body)

Let me explain. For centuries, scientists have believed that energy and mass are completely unrelated to each other. But I wondered... what if they are one and the same? Mass could be turned into energy and energy into mass.

To find the amount of energy, my ingenious equation multiplies mass by the speed of light, squared. The speed of light is a vast quantity, and when it's squared, it is unbelievably gigantic. So my equation shows that even a teeny-weeny atom-size mass can generate an absolutely massive amount of energy. Just between you and me, diary, I think I deserve a big pat on the back.

But tonight, the year ends. What might my equation mean for the future? The industrial age is at its peak right now, but we need to harness even more energy. Some day, could we release the energy locked inside mass to power the world? Goodbye for now, my diary.

1911

Dear diary, I haven't forgotten you. I've been so busy the past six years and there are so many amazing developments to ponder. This year my brilliant colleague at Cambridge University, Ernest Rutherford, suggested that an atom has a hard core with a positive charge that contains almost all of its mass (you haven't forgotten mass from my equation...). And that a cloud of tiny electrons with a small amount of mass and a negative charge orbit the core. Smart stuff.

## 1932

Dear diary, old friend, can you ever forgive me for being so long out of touch? These are such exciting times. Rutherford's colleague James Chadwick has discovered that the nucleus (that's the name for an atom's core) contains particles with no charge, called neutrons.

Nucleus

Electron

## 1933

Diary! We're on the brink of something... Hungarian physicist Leo Szilard had a brain wave while waiting for a red light to change: if the nucleus of an atom contains mass, would it be possible to split it to get energy from it? If so, and we had a number of atoms, and the energy from each nucleus was released in a chain reaction (a process they've called nuclear fission), would a huge, devastating amount of energy be released...? That would certainly be a traffic stopper!

## 1939

Oh dear, diary. Szilard's been in touch. Some German scientists worked on a fission experiment last year (they bombarded a uranium atom with neutrons until the atom split), and, just as he'd predicted, mighty amounts of energy were released in an explosion. Szilard's writing a letter here in the States to President Roosevelt to explain how devastating nuclear (named after the nucleus) bombs might be. He wants me to sign the letter, as it needs to get the attention it deserves (and I'm quite a big deal these days, what with a Nobel Prize in physics under my belt an all). I do hope the president heeds the warning. It was only an equation, after all. I didn't mean it to lead to something so dangerous.

President Franklin D. Roosevelt
The White House
Washington, D.C.
U.S.A.

# JOURNEYS

Feeling up in the air or out to sea? Maybe it's time to leave the safety of solid ground behind and journey into the skies or across the oceans. Imagine the perils the first aviators faced as they chased the dream of human flight. Consider the danger of setting sail for unknown waters towards some distant destination. Find out how to be a highflier, as well as learning what floats your boat.

## Early flight

In 1783, the French Montgolfier brothers rose up into the sky in an unsteerable hot-air balloon. By the 1890s, a pair of German brothers, Otto and Gustav Lilienthal, made steerable flights in gliders. Close on their tail in 1903, yet another brother team, Orville and Wilbur Wright, made the first controlled and powered aircraft flight. We had liftoff!

## Taking flight

Aircraft stay in the air because of four basic forces: lift (going up), weight (pulling down), thrust (moving ahead), and drag (resisting motion). In order for aircraft to fly straight and level at a constant speed, the forces must act in pairs. That means thrust must be equal to drag and lift must be equal to weight.

**Lift**
The force that acts to push the aircraft up is called lift. The way air moves around the wings, together with the shape of the wings, give the aircraft lift. Up, up, and away!

**Drag**
The force that resists the motion of a moving object and slows it down is called drag. Aircraft are designed to let air pass around them with less drag.

**Weight**
The force that pulls the aircraft back to Earth is weight. Aircraft are heavy, but they are constructed so that their weight is spread from front to back, keeping everything balanced.

**Thrust**
Propellers or jet engines create powerful thrust to move the aircraft forward to its destination. Fire up all cylinders!

## Air crashes

What happens when something goes wrong? Thankfully, most air crashes are not fatal. Between 1980 and 2000, for example, there were 568 plane crashes in the U.S., and 90 percent of the victims survived. To improve your chances, it's worth knowing that passengers in the rear of the plane are 40 percent more likely to survive a crash.

## Maritime navigation

Boats have been around for a very long time, and navigation as a science is at least 5,000 years old. The astrolabe (an instrument used in navigation that showed the positions of the planets and stars at a given time) was highly developed in the Islamic world by 800 CE. About 200 years later, the Chinese were using a magnetic compass for navigation. By the time the great age of exploration ended in the early 17th century, ships and navigators were advanced and experienced enough to sail just about anywhere in the world.

## Shipwrecks

What sinks a ship? Taking on water is an obvious problem—large waves can break over the sides of a vessel, and leaks can let water in. Storms can toss a ship against the rocks, while a navigation error resulting in a crash can cause rips in the hull that let water pour in. Plug up the holes and ensure that more water is going out than pouring in or you'll soon get that sinking feeling

## Staying afloat

Boats float using pairs of forces, too: buoyancy (pushing up), weight (pushing down), thrust (moving forward), and drag (resisting motion). An object in water will float if it displaces an amount of water equal to its own weight; if a boat weighs 2,200 lb (1,000 kg), it will sink until it has displaced 2,200 lb (1,000 kg) of water. A boat's average density is light compared to water, so very little of it must submerge before it has displaced its weight.

An equal weight of displaced water pushes up against the boat to make it float. As long as the boat is stable and the weight of its passengers and cargo is distributed evenly, it will float safely.

**Drag**

**Buoyancy**

**Thrust**

**Weight**

*The weight of the boat pushes down against the water to displace it.*

## FORCES OF ENERGY

Energy and forces go hand in hand in making things move and stop. Movement (kinetic) energy is what makes a car go. If the car should then crash into a concrete wall, the wall acts as an opposing force on the car. If the wall's mass is bigger than the car's mass and speed, it will bring the car to a crashing halt. But the kinetic energy doesn't just disappear when the car stops; it turns into several other forms...

Heat energy is released from the crash as a converted form of the kinetic energy that was driving the car forward. Think how hot your bicycle brakes feel when you stop suddenly.

CRASH

BANG

The force with which the wall "hits" the car is equal to that with which the car hits the wall to bring the car to a standstill. In a crash with a stationary object, a car's speed drops to zero in under a second.

Bending and crushing parts of the car body use up some of the kinetic energy, and more energy is used in creating the sound of the crash.

CRUMPLE ZONE

## CRASH COURSE

Good morning, class. Today's lesson looks at how cars withstand impact and keep passengers safe. It's been more than 100 years since the first car-accident casualty. Since then, an estimated 20 million people have died in car-related incidents. As a crash-test dummy, I know all about bumpy rides. Buckle up!

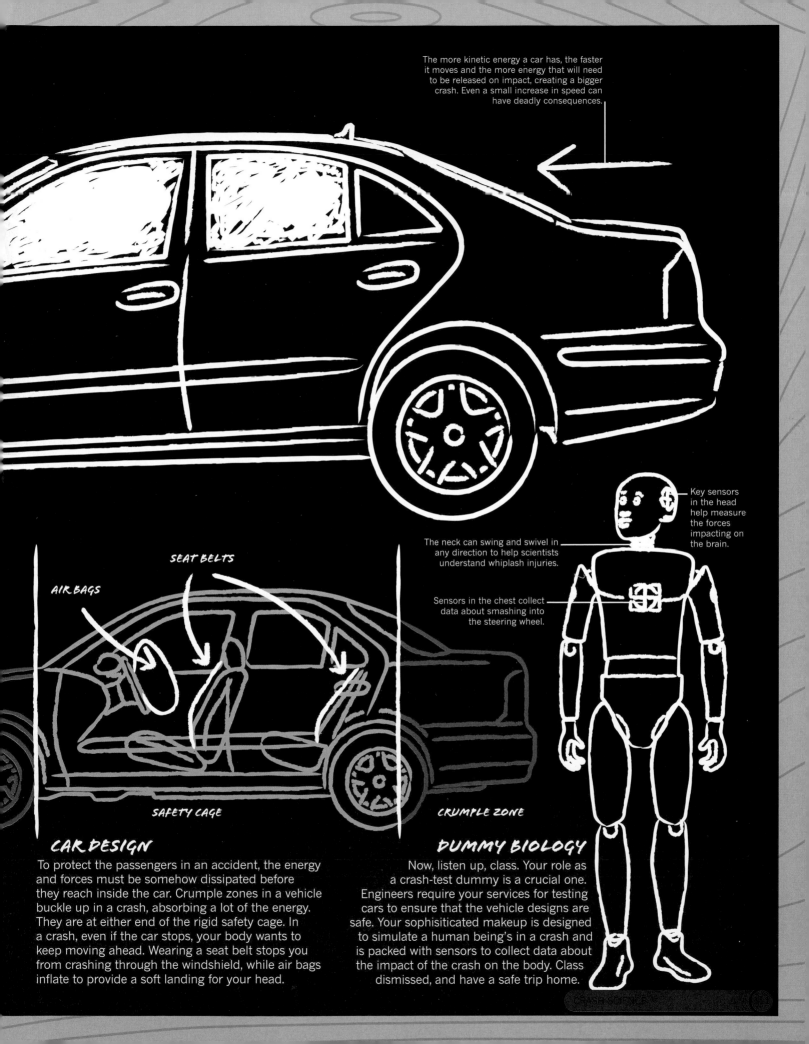

The more kinetic energy a car has, the faster it moves and the more energy that will need to be released on impact, creating a bigger crash. Even a small increase in speed can have deadly consequences.

Key sensors in the head help measure the forces impacting on the brain.

The neck can swing and swivel in any direction to help scientists understand whiplash injuries.

Sensors in the chest collect data about smashing into the steering wheel.

AIR BAGS

SEAT BELTS

SAFETY CAGE

CRUMPLE ZONE

## CAR DESIGN

To protect the passengers in an accident, the energy and forces must be somehow dissipated before they reach inside the car. Crumple zones in a vehicle buckle up in a crash, absorbing a lot of the energy. They are at either end of the rigid safety cage. In a crash, even if the car stops, your body wants to keep moving ahead. Wearing a seat belt stops you from crashing through the windshield, while air bags inflate to provide a soft landing for your head.

## DUMMY BIOLOGY

Now, listen up, class. Your role as a crash-test dummy is a crucial one. Engineers require your services for testing cars to ensure that the vehicle designs are safe. Your sophisiticated makeup is designed to simulate a human being's in a crash and is packed with sensors to collect data about the impact of the crash on the body. Class dismissed, and have a safe trip home.

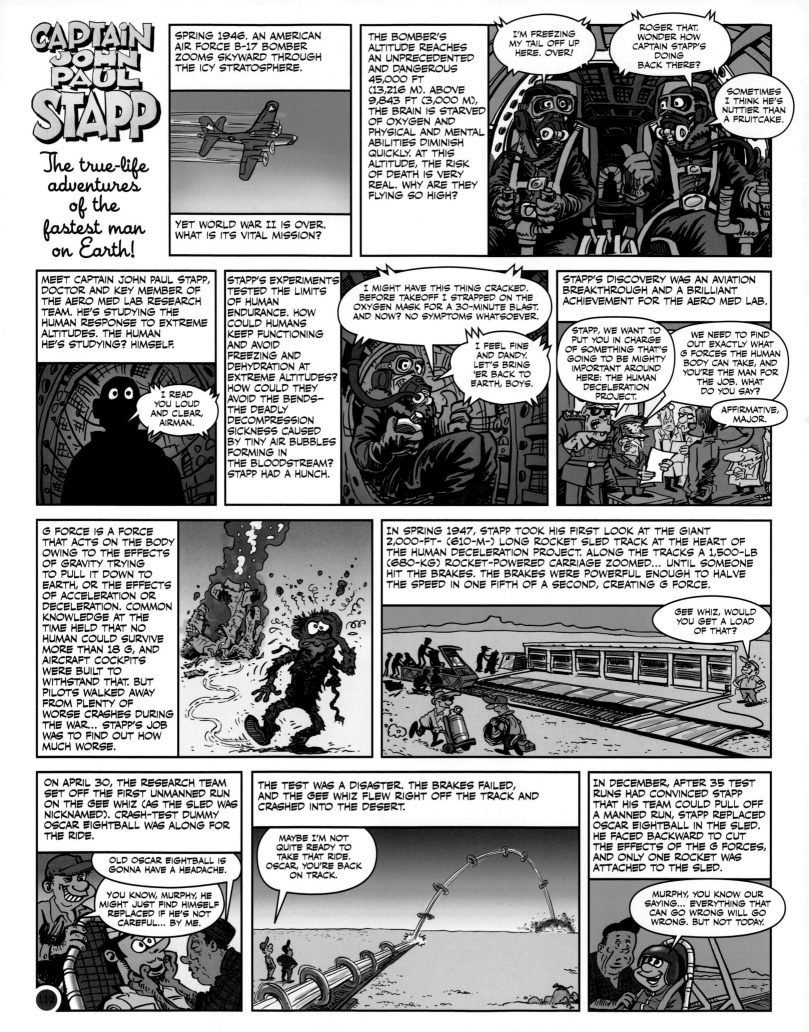

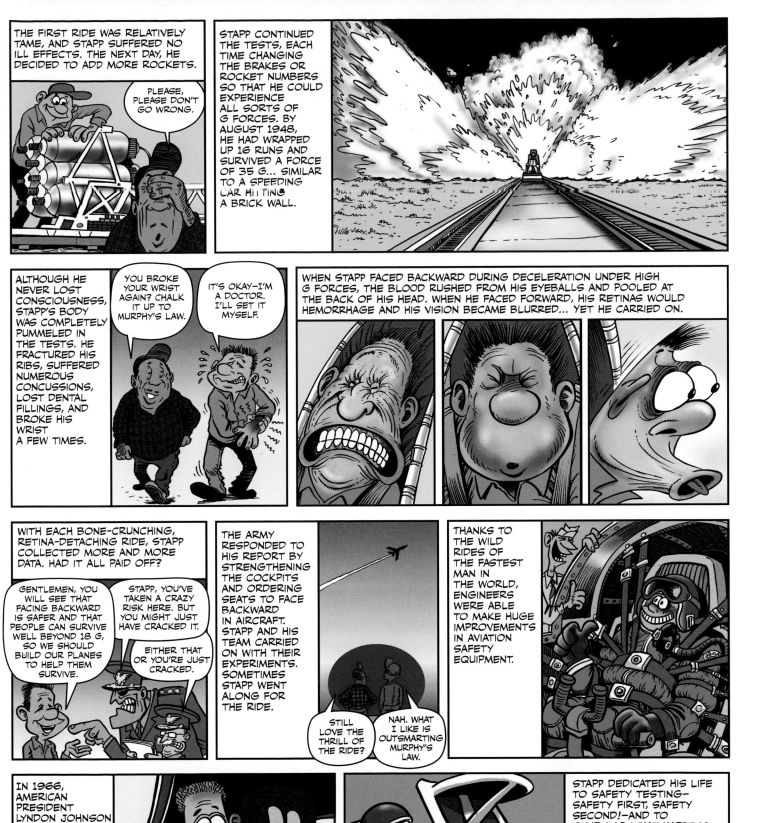

# HUMAN BODY HORRORS

The world is full of beastly bugs just waiting to invade your body. From pathogens under your fingernails to parasites in your bed, they hide in the most everyday places. But your body is no pushover for these microscopic monsters. Discover its strategies for survival on the biological battlefield of life.

# HORRIBLE HANDSCAPE

Hands and fingers are very useful for picking up objects, but they also pick up bacteria and viruses that can cause disease. These invaders turn your palms into their playground, joining the resident germs that usually live there harmlessly.

### Rhinovirus

This virus causes colds, and you can pick it up, packaged in slimy mucus, by touching something that an infected person has sneezed on. If you then touch your nose or mouth, it won't be long before you'll have a cold, too.

### Flu virus

Fever, muscle pains, a sore throat, and headaches are what's in store if you come into contact with this virus. Touch a contaminated surface and then touch your mouth or nose, and you might end up with a real pain in the neck.

### Salmonella

Salmonella is one nasty bacterium found especially on raw chicken. If you get it on your hands or food preparation surfaces, it can contaminate your food, giving you stomach cramps and a horrible case of diarrhea.

### Norovirus

A common cause of bad stomach upsets, the norovirus spreads like wildfire from person to person. If you use a toilet where someone who is infected has just vomited or had diarrhea and don't wash your hands, you'll be next!

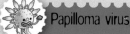
### Papilloma virus

These little critters actually get into the skin and make its cells multiply. The result is a bump on the skin's surface that often resembles a mini cauliflower and is better known as a wart. Who wants a handshake?

### Staphylococcus

This bacterium usually lives harmlessly on your skin or up your nose. But some strains can cause nasty boils on the skin or lead to blood poisoning and meningitis. One very good reason not to pick your nose!

### E. coli

Most types of *Escherichia coli* (E. coli) live harmlessly in your colon. However, harmful strains picked up from undercooked meat or transferred by touch from person to person can cause all sorts of diseases, from meningitis in newborn babies to diarrhea.

### Propionibacterium

Here's a bacterium that lives on the skin's surface as a permanent resident, sliding down pores to feed in the skin's oil-producing sebaceous glands. If pores get blocked and trap this bacterium inside, it multiplies, causing swelling that produces sore pimples called acne.

## Hand hygiene

Feeling grossed out? To remove these unseen nasties and reduce the risk of infection, regularly wash your hands—especially after you go to the bathroom, before you eat or prepare food, and after handling money. Use warm water and soap and rub your hands together for 20 seconds, making sure you scrub under your fingernails and in between your fingers. Then thoroughly dry your hands on a clean towel; damp hands are a breeding ground for germs.

**Handy hiding place**
Many people wear rings, and some people never take theirs off. But just one ring can harbor hundreds of millions of bacteria and viruses, shielding them from cleansing soap suds. Run rings around these germ hideouts by washing your jewelry once a week.

# DESTINATION: HUMAN

Hustling and bustling their way through the station, these pesky parasites are on their way to a human body near you. Once they reach their destination, parasites take what they want from the body, feeding and breeding on or in it. They are the worst kinds of tourists, causing irritation or illness to the local host. Eavesdrop on their chat to see where they are headed.

| Time | Platform | To |
|---|---|---|
| 10:05 | 5 | MOUTH JUNCTION (change for onward connections to Colon and Small Intestine) |
| 10:22 | 1 | EYES (via Blood) |
| 10:31 | 6 | BRAIN CAPITAL (via Blood) |
| 10:52 | 4 | SKIN GATEWAY |
| 10:55 | 3 | LIVER (sushi cart available onboard) |
| 11:02 | 9 | LEGS ROAD |
| 11:30 | 8 | SCALP CITY (via Hair) |

## African eye worm

Nice to chat, but that's my train, and I need to hitch a ride with a mango fly onboard. Hopefully, the trip will make the fly hungry so that when it feeds, it will inject my larvae into its human host. Once in, they'll mature into worms and then catch the blood highway to the eyes, where they wiggle around and can be a real pain!

## Pinworm

Hi! I'm just back from the colon. Life there was perfect for a roundworm like me because it's dark, slimy, and warm. When I was full of eggs, I just wormed my way out through the anus. That made it itchy, so my eggs got scratched up by the unlucky human and delivered to the mouth. They're now on their way to the colon.

## Ascaris

You sound like a meanie to me, Trypanosoma. I don't usually cause too much harm, unless there's a big group of us and we block the small intestine. Today, I'm just dropping off the kids. Still tiny eggs, they're also on their way to the mouth where they'll catch a connection through the digestive system to the small intestine.

## Trypanosoma brucei

I'm just a microscopic protozoan (single-celled organism) waiting for the Tsetse Fly Express to take me directly to the bloodstream. Then I'll move on to the brain and give it the deadly sleeping sickness. Yawn.

Unt. . NNX 04.05.07

EYES

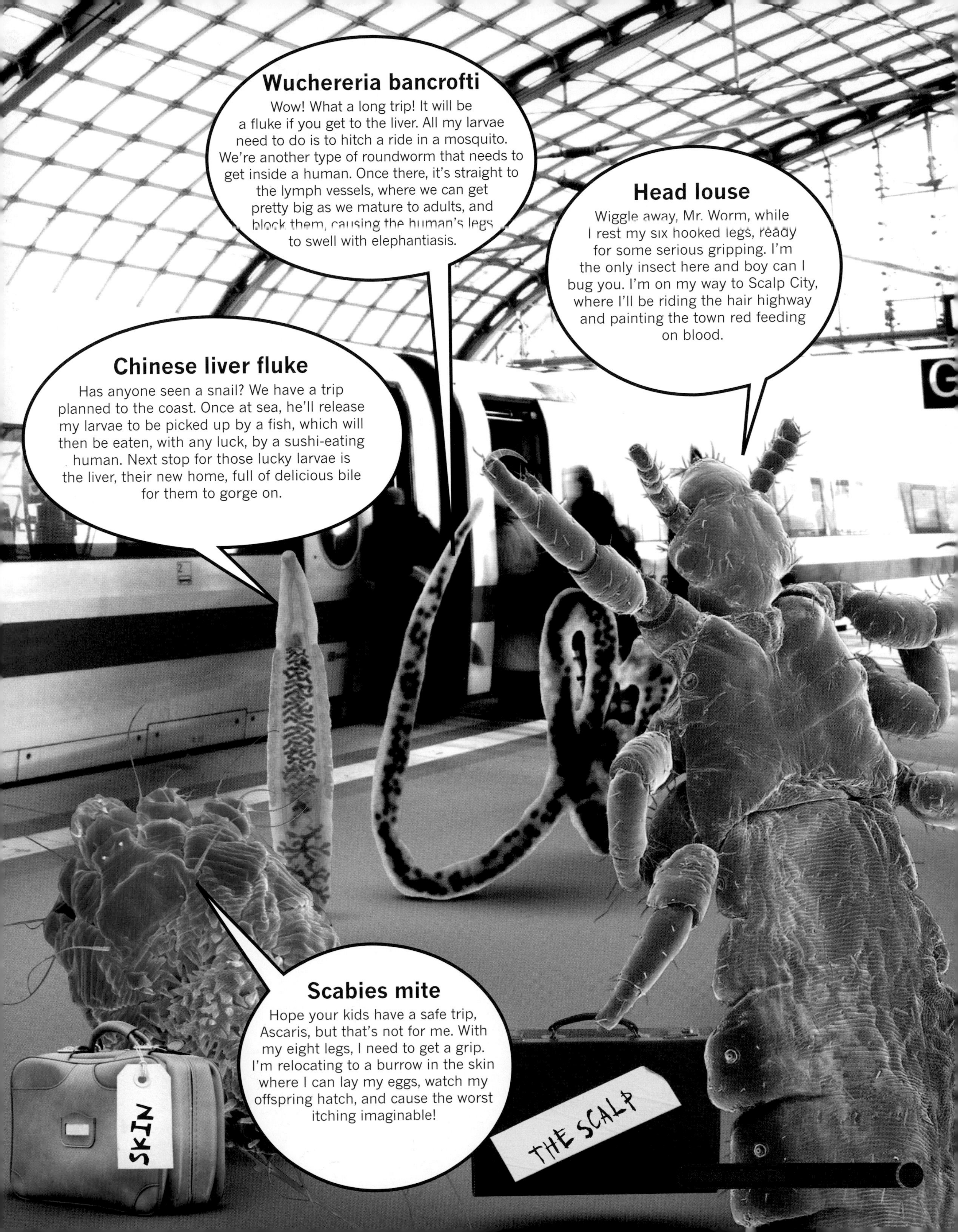
Wuchereria bancrofti
Wow! What a long trip! It will be a fluke if you get to the liver. All my larvae need to do is to hitch a ride in a mosquito. We're another type of roundworm that needs to get inside a human. Once there, it's straight to the lymph vessels, where we can get pretty big as we mature to adults, and block them, causing the human's legs to swell with elephantiasis.
Head louse
Wiggle away, Mr. Worm, while I rest my six hooked legs, ready for some serious gripping. I'm the only insect here and boy can I bug you. I'm on my way to Scalp City, where I'll be riding the hair highway and painting the town red feeding on blood.
Chinese liver fluke
Has anyone seen a snail? We have a trip planned to the coast. Once at sea, he'll release my larvae to be picked up by a fish, which will then be eaten, with any luck, by a sushi-eating human. Next stop for those lucky larvae is the liver, their new home, full of delicious bile for them to gorge on.
Scabies mite
Hope your kids have a safe trip, Ascaris, but that's not for me. With my eight legs, I need to get a grip. I'm relocating to a burrow in the skin where I can lay my eggs, watch my offspring hatch, and cause the worst itching imaginable!
SKIN
THE SCALP

# UNDER ATTACK

Threatened by attack from a team of disease-causing pathogens, the body's defense team is fielding a squad of germ bashers. The defenders will have to be on their toes to try to get into as bacteria, viruses, and other heavyweights attackers are body tissues and cause mayhem. But those attackers try to get into facing strong defense tactics and the game will be tough.

## Bacteria

Battling bacteria are key players on the attack team. Once they get a foothold inside the body, bacteria release toxins that either kill body cells or stop them from working properly. Allow them to advance and bacteria can cause diseases such as meningitis and pneumonia.

## Fungi

There are some harmful fungi on the attack squad—and they are not fun guys at all. Those that cause athlete's foot and ringworm invade and grow through the skin, feeding on living tissues and making the skin cracked, red, and sore.

## Viruses

The most aggressive members of the attack team, viruses have a special way of infecting the body. Left unchallenged, they invade body cells and make multiple copies of themselves before seeking new cells to invade. Colds, the flu, measles, and rabies are all caused by viruses.

## Protists

Many protists, such as pond-dwelling amebas, are completely harmless, but some have been recruited to the pathogen squad. Giardia, for example, picked up from infested food and water, irritates the intestines and causes vile, stinking diarrhea.

## B cells

Along with the killer T cells, B cells form the brains of the defense team. They pinpoint and target key players in the attack team. B cells release chemicals called antibodies that disable specific bacteria and other pathogens, making them easier targets for their phagocyte teammates.

## Antibiotics

However good the defense team is, it needs a little outside support to help it achieve the ultimate victory. That support comes in the form of powerful drugs antibiotics. These are powerful drugs on antibiotics. These go straight for the bacteria on the opposing team and stop them from multiplying inside the body. No multiplication, no infection!

## Superbugs

Superbugs are the players to fear the most. They are bacteria that have become resistant to antibiotics on the defense team. MRSA is a superbug that can cause serious skin infections, especially when a person's natural defense is weakened.

## Killer T cells

These are the specialists on the defense team that make a beeline for attacking viruses on the other team. More specifically, killer T cells seek out body cells with viruses that are about to multiply inside them. Killer T cells stick to these body cells, punch holes in them, and release chemicals that finish off the attackers.

## Phagocytes

These guys pack a real punch. Phagocytes are first into the fray and do their best to knock down the attack team. These are the defense cells that grab ahold of pathogens, eat them up, and destroy them. The nimblest are the neutrophils, but the more powerful are the extremely hungry macrophages.

## Vaccines

Every team needs a trainer, and that's exactly what vaccines do for the defense squad. They prime the B cells and T cells so that they are ready from the start to launch a full-scale assault on the nastiest pathogens on the attack team, such as those that cause measles and mumps, before they can do any damage.

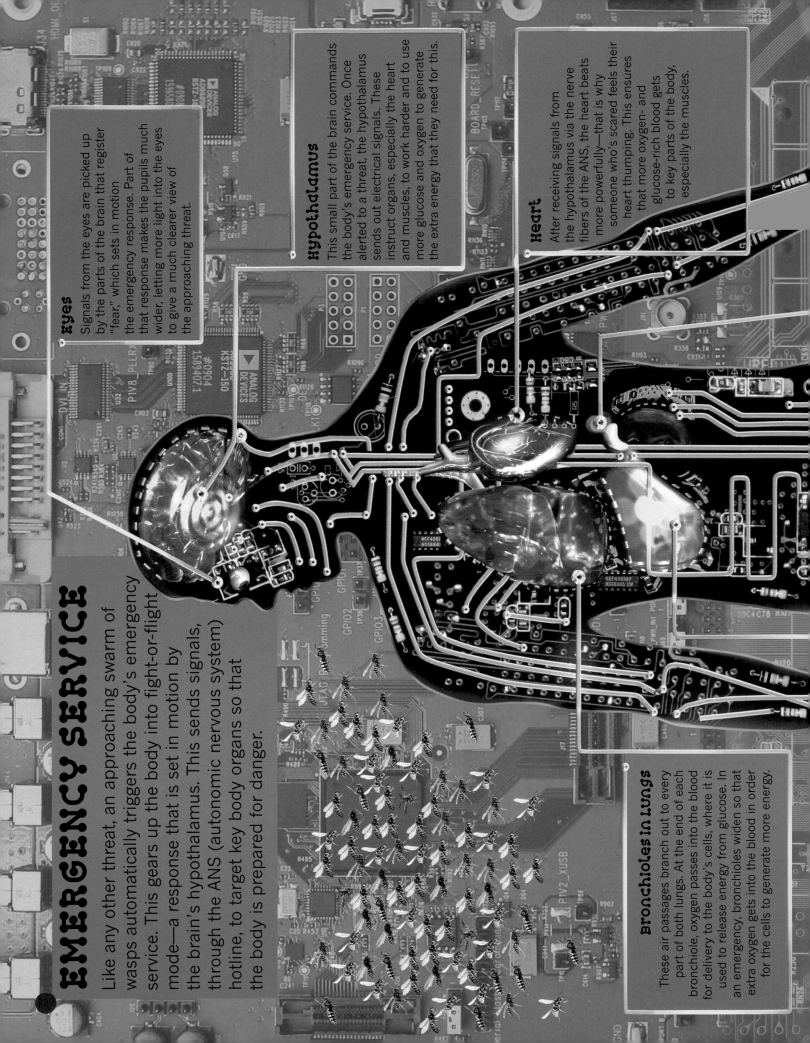

# EMERGENCY SERVICE

Like any other threat, an approaching swarm of wasps automatically triggers the body's emergency service. This gears up the body into fight-or-flight mode—a response that is set in motion by the brain's hypothalamus. This sends signals, through the ANS (autonomic nervous system) hotline, to target key body organs so that the body is prepared for danger.

## Eyes

Signals from the eyes are picked up by the parts of the brain that register "fear," which sets in motion the emergency response. Part of that response makes the pupils much wider, letting more light into the eyes to give a much clearer view of the approaching threat.

## Hypothalamus

This small part of the brain commands the body's emergency service. Once alerted to a threat, the hypothalamus sends out electrical signals. These instruct organs, especially the heart and muscles, to work harder and to use more glucose and oxygen to generate the extra energy that they need for this.

## Heart

After receiving signals from the hypothalamus via the nerve fibers of the ANS, the heart beats more powerfully—that is why someone who's scared feels their heart thumping. This ensures that more oxygen- and glucose-rich blood gets to key parts of the body, especially the muscles.

## Bronchioles in Lungs

These air passages branch out to every part of both lungs. At the end of each bronchiole, oxygen passes into the blood for delivery to the body's cells, where it is used to release energy from glucose. In an emergency, bronchioles widen so that extra oxygen gets into the blood in order for the cells to generate more energy.

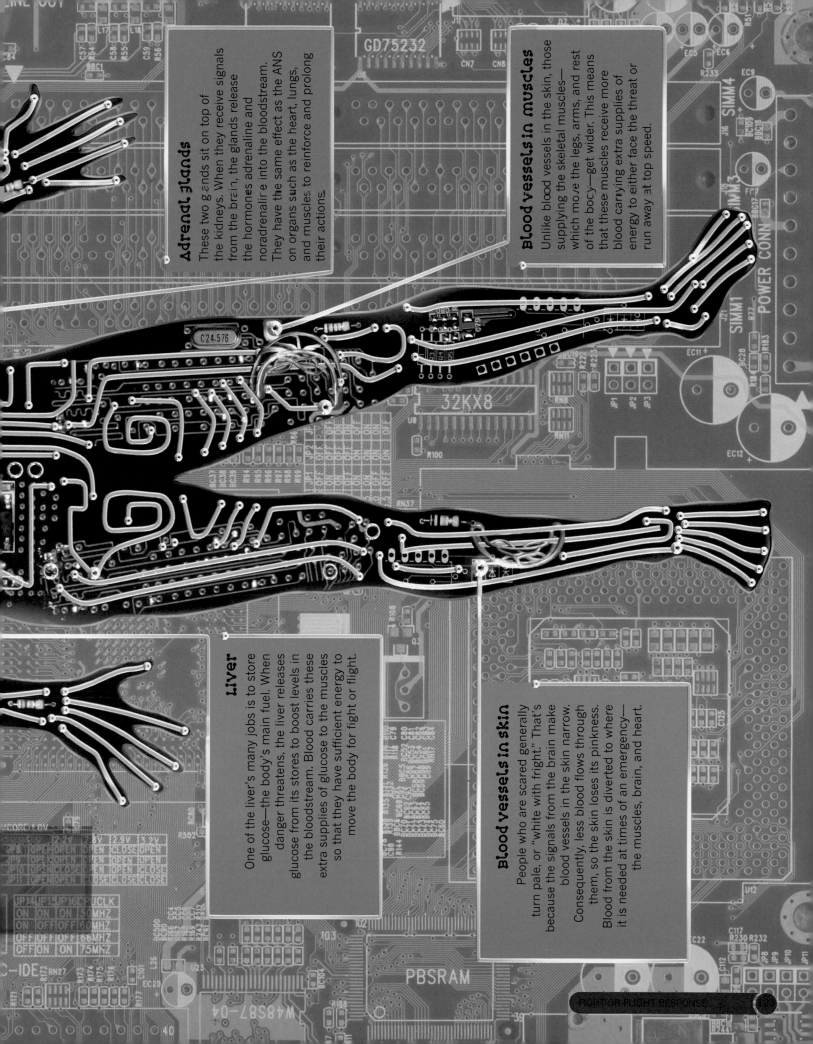

## Adrenal glands

These two glands sit on top of the kidneys. When they receive signals from the brain, the glands release the hormones adrenaline and noradrenaline into the bloodstream. They have the same effect as the ANS on organs such as the heart, lungs, and muscles to reinforce and prolong their actions.

## Blood vessels in muscles

Unlike blood vessels in the skin, those supplying the skeletal muscles—which move the legs, arms, and rest of the body—get wider. This means that these muscles receive more blood carrying extra supplies of energy to either face the threat or run away at top speed.

## Liver

One of the liver's many jobs is to store glucose—the body's main fuel. When danger threatens, the liver releases glucose from its stores to boost levels in the bloodstream. Blood carries these extra supplies of glucose to the muscles so that they have sufficient energy to move the body for fight or flight.

## Blood vessels in skin

People who are scared generally turn pale, or "white with fright." That's because the signals from the brain make blood vessels in the skin narrow. Consequently, less blood flows through them, so the skin loses its pinkness. Blood from the skin is diverted to where it is needed at times of an emergency—the muscles, brain, and heart.

# OUTBREAK!

Ever since people started living in large groups, they have been attacked by outbreaks of disease. Epidemics affect whole communities, while pandemics spread around the world. What made them more fearful was that no one had any idea what caused them. Today, we know that outbreaks of disease are caused by pathogens (germs) such as bacteria and viruses. But even with this knowledge, we are still vulnerable to attack.

## SMALLPOX HITS THE NEW WORLD

The invasion of the "New World" by conquistadors—adventurers and soldiers from Spain and Portugal—has been a disaster for the Native American peoples. Since they arrived in the 15th century in search of gold and silver, the Europeans have spread diseases to which the native peoples have no resistance. The most deadly of these is smallpox—a viral disease that has already killed millions.

**Native Americans hurl projectiles at armed Spanish conquistadors.**

## NAPOLEON'S ARMY FALLS

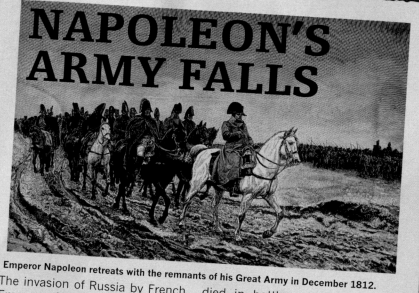

**Emperor Napoleon retreats with the remnants of his Great Army in December 1812.**

The invasion of Russia by French Emperor Napoleon Bonaparte's Great Army that began in April 1812 has ended in disaster. Of the 500,000 soldiers who headed for Moscow, only 40,000 survivors have returned to France. Many died in battle and from bitter cold and starvation, but most were killed by an epidemic of typhus. This disease is rapidly spread—especially in cramped and unsanitary conditions—by bloodsucking body lice.

## BLACK DEATH

In only four years, the Black Death has spread across Europe, wiping out one half of the population. This dreadful disease, first reported in 1347, causes a high temperature, bloody black sores, and a painful death. It is believed to be bubonic plague—a disease caused by bacteria that is passed to humans by fleas that bite infected rats.

**Two victims of the Black Death reveal the horrible sores that cover their bodies.**

## CHOLERA

The 19th century has seen several pandemics of this disease. Spread by food and water contaminated with bacteria, cholera causes diarrhea and vomiting and often kills its victims. It first arrived in Europe from India in 1817 and by the 1830s had spread to the Americas. Cholera is more likely to occur in cities where sanitation is poor and drinking water dirty.

**Two public disinfectors pull their cart to a new location to tackle another outbreak of cholera.**

# "SPANISH" FLU

When World War I ended in November 1918, it had claimed millions of victims, but much fewer than the influenza pandemic that struck that same year. Caused by a virus, "Spanish" flu targeted healthy young adults and could kill within hours. It spread across the globe with breathtaking speed, killing more than 50 million people before it disappeared in 1919.

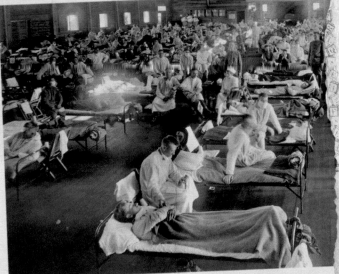

Doctors and nurses tend patients in an emergency ward set up to cope with Spanish flu victims. This ward is based at the U.S. Army's camp in Kansas.

# EBOLA FEVER

The first outbreak of this killer disease was in the Democratic Republic of the Congo in 1976. There have been other outbreaks since then, but only ever in Africa. Highly contagious, Ebola is caused by a virus transmitted through saliva, blood, and other bodily fluids. It results in internal bleeding and is usually fatal.

## Severe Acute Respiratory Syndrome

Air travel seems to be "helping" the spread of this new, and potentially fatal, disease around the world. First reported in the Chinese province of Guangdong in 2002, SARS is a viral disease that is initially picked up from wild animals. It causes breathing difficulties, fatigue, and diarrhea. In only two years, more than 8,000 people have been infected.

Hong Kong residents wear masks to reduce the risk of picking up the virus that causes SARS.

# AIDS—CURE HOPE

The pandemic of acquired immunodeficiency syndrome (AIDS) first emerged in 1981. Two years later, its cause was identified as human immunodeficiency virus, or HIV. Spread by bodily fluids, such as blood, the virus invades key defense cells, known as helper T cells. This weakens the immune system and the body falls prey to various diseases. Research is still under way to find a cure for this international killer.

HIV viruses (green) erupt from helper T cells before invading and multiplying inside more of these defense cells.

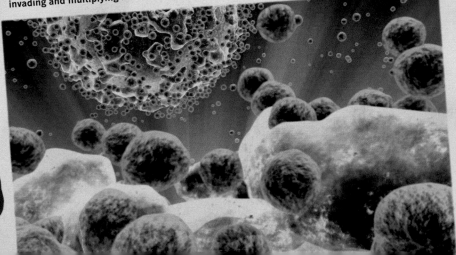

# MEASLES OUTBREAK IN JAPAN

The measles epidemic that has affected thousands of students and spread rapidly through Tokyo in May 2007 has taken health officials by surprise. Highly contagious, and usually affecting young children, the measles virus is spread by coughs and sneezes. It can occasionally be fatal. The outbreak is being blamed on Japan's failure to vaccinate all children against the disease.

### Leap of faith

Look skyward to witness the true terror of land diving—a ritual performed in the Pacific nation of Vanuatu to ensure a good harvest or to impress girlfriends! With a vine attached to each ankle, this young man leaps from a rickety tower. If he's lucky, his head will miss the ground!

### Outstanding display

Be amazed by the khareshwari, or "standing baba." He's an Indian holy man who has vowed to stand, without sitting or lying down, for an incredible 12 years! A swing supports him whether he's awake or asleep, and he can rest one leg at a time in a sling.

### Fire-walking feat

Taking center stage, our star turn walks barefoot over hot embers without getting burned. How does she do it? The trick is that ashy coals are poor conductors of heat, and because she walks quickly, there's not enough contact with individual coals to burn her feet.

# HOW TOUGH ARE YOU?

The circus is in town! Come and marvel at displays of human strength and endurance. Witness our performers pushing their bodies to the limits. Gasp as they tolerate extremes of heat, cold, pain, and pressure. These are tough acts to follow.

## Manjit the magnificent

Entering stage right, dragging a double-decker bus, is Indian-born Manjit Singh. In 2009, the magnificent Manjit used his incredible power, and his superstrong hair, to pull a bus weighing 9.5 tons (8.6 tonnes) for more than 70 ft (21 m) through a London park. Hair-raising!

## Bed of nails

Never failing to impress, this fearless performer rests on a bed of nails without bleeding or writhing in pain. His body weight is distributed over hundreds of nails, so the downward pressure at any one point is not enough to pierce his skin.

## Meditating monk

If you were in this ice bath, draped in freezing wet sheets, your body temperature would plummet and you would eventually die. But in his state of deep meditation, the monk generates enough heat to stay warm inside—and even to make the sheets steam as his bath water evaporates. Cool stuff!

# RISKY BUSINESS

Food is essential for life—but eating it carries certain risks. Some foods, especially those that are processed, contain added ingredients or unwanted pollutants that may affect your health. Food may even be contaminated or made with ingredients that you would rather not know about... To find out more, check out the Grim Foods supermarket. You'll be surprised what's in our food!

**ALWAYS WASH FOOD BEFORE EATING!**

99¢

## MELAMINE IN MILK

You would expect baby's milk powder to be safe. But, in China in 2008, some powders were tainted with melamine—a poisonous substance that makes the product appear to contain more protein than it actually does. Melamine poisons children, causing kidney problems and sometimes death.

## PESTICIDES

At least five pieces of fruit and vegetables a day are recommended as part of a healthy diet. However, those "healthy" components of the diet may also carry traces of poisonous pesticides that were sprayed on them while they were growing to kill pests.

78¢

### TUNA

Whether canned or fresh, tuna is a popular food. It's also good for the brain and heart. But tuna may contain traces of toxic heavy metals, such as mercury, that pollute the oceans and that can cause health problems. That's why it's recommended that we eat tuna no more than twice a week.

### TRANS FATS

Man-made trans fats are used in the manufacture of many processed foods, including cookies, bread, and microwave meals. This is because they add bulk and give the products a longer shelf life. Unfortunately, they can increase the risk of heart attacks and strokes if eaten in large amounts.

## ENTER NOW—IT'S DEAD EASY!

Contestants are required to eat as much of one type of food as possible in a fixed time.

Choose from:
chicken wings
asparagus
pancakes

**WARNING:** A Russian man collapsed and died after gorging on 43 cream-and-banana pancakes. People are at risk of choking on excess food lodged in the throat.

## Staying alive water warning

None of us can survive for long without water. We need to drink it to replace water lost daily in sweat, urine, and so on. But drinking excessive amounts of water may be dangerous. It can dilute the blood and make brain cells expand, causing coma, convulsions, and even death.

YOU'LL REAP YOUR REWARD FOR HEALTHY EATING...

$1.99

SPECIAL GRISTLE OFFER

## HAMBURGERS

There have been cases where cheap hamburgers, contaminated with a lethal strain of E. coli bacteria and served undercooked, caused severe illness in children. And in some places, the cattle that produce hamburger beef are given growth-boosting hormones that can affect children's development.

## Grim Jim's quote of the day:

*"Think before you eat or you'll be dead on your feet!"*

80¢

High salt content!

## SALT

A long list of processed foods contain added salt as a flavor enhancer to make them tastier. These foods include ketchup, pizzas, baked beans, chips, microwave meals, soups, and bread. In adults, eating too much salt can increase blood pressure and also the risk of having a heart attack.

$1.10

## HOT DOGS

Next time you dig into a hot dog or another cheap meat product, think about this: it may contain mechanically recovered meat. This is made from ground-up pieces of fatty meat, gristle, and tissue left behind on a carcass once the valuable meat has been removed. Bon appetit!

# BIZARRE ER

What has happened to bring these people to the hospital's emergency room (ER)? Some of them are accident prone, while others are just unlucky. Doctors working here find out what happened, investigate the nature of the injury, and either patch the patient up or send them off for further treatment by a specialist.

The accidents here may sound bizarre, but most are surprisingly common.

## Swallowing objects

From door keys to silverware, false teeth to batteries, people swallow the strangest things. On arrival in ER, doctors send the patient to be x-rayed, which will identify what has been swallowed. Most small objects, such as coins, pass safely through the body, but sharp objects, such as open safety pins, can be life threatening.

## Machinery accidents

Despite strict safety regulations, people arrive in ER time and time again as a result of workplace accidents involving machinery, which can cause cuts, burns, or broken bones and severed fingers. Injuries often require immediate surgery to prevent infection or the loss of a limb.

## Cheerleading

Once it was just pompons and high kicks, but modern cheerleading is a dangerous sport. Displays involve such gymnastic stunts and tricks as human pyramids and flip jumps. Just one wrong foot can result in broken bones, a concussion, or even paralysis.

## Left-handed tools

Only 10 percent of the population are left-handed, and they arrive in ER with injuries caused by using tools designed for right-handers. Even ordinary scissors, used by a left-hander, can more easily slip and cause cuts or stab wounds.

## Lightning strikes

When a bolt of lightning hits the ground, the strike may also hit people, causing burns or damage to the nervous system. Doctors in ER assess the injury and organize appropriate treatment. The good news is that there is only a one in three million chance of being struck by lightning.

## Falling out of bed

It's surprising how many people suffer bumps, bruises, cuts, and fractures and end up in ER after falling out of bed. Many are older people with a poor sense of balance. Young children are also experts at falling out of bed.

## Party poppers

Pull the string and a tiny charge inside a party popper shoots streamers into the air. But accidents caused by party poppers are no cause for celebration. Doctors in ER regularly see both adults and children who have been hit in the eye by the cap that flies off when the popper pops.

## Charging cows

Walking in the country near a field of cows should not cause problems. But cattle may react if they feel threatened, especially if they have calves to protect. Walkers, often those with dogs, have been charged and trampled by cows, arriving in ER with serious, and sometimes fatal, injuries.

## Falling coconuts

What could be more idyllic than tall coconut palms along a sandy beach? But those palm trees can also pose a danger. Coconuts weigh up to 8.8 lb (4 kg), and may fall from a height of 82 ft (25 m) to the ground. Anyone hit by a falling coconut could end up in ER with a concussion or even brain damage.

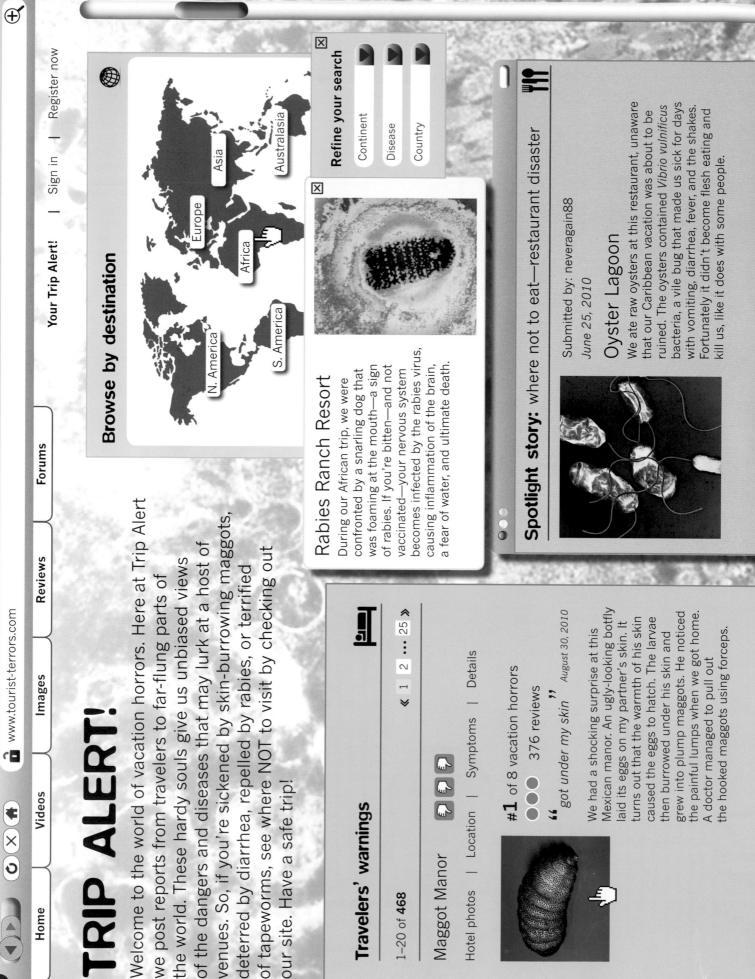

www.tourist-terrors.com

Home | Videos | Images | Reviews | Forums

Your Trip Alert!   |   Sign in   |   Register now

# TRIP ALERT!

Welcome to the world of vacation horrors. Here at Trip Alert we post reports from travelers to far-flung parts of the world. These hardy souls give us unbiased views of the dangers and diseases that may lurk at a host of venues. So, if you're sickened by skin-burrowing maggots, deterred by diarrhea, repelled by rabies, or terrified of tapeworms, see where NOT to visit by checking out our site. Have a safe trip!

## Browse by destination

N. America

S. America

Europe

Africa

Asia

Australasia

## Refine your search

Continent

Disease

Country

## Rabies Ranch Resort

During our African trip, we were confronted by a snarling dog that was foaming at the mouth—a sign of rabies. If you're bitten—and not vaccinated—your nervous system becomes infected by the rabies virus, causing inflammation of the brain, a fear of water, and ultimate death.

## Spotlight story: where not to eat—restaurant disaster

Submitted by: neveragain88
*June 25, 2010*

### Oyster Lagoon

We ate raw oysters at this restaurant, unaware that our Caribbean vacation was about to be ruined. The oysters contained *Vibrio vulnificus* bacteria, a vile bug that made us sick for days with vomiting, diarrhea, fever, and the shakes. Fortunately it didn't become flesh eating and kill us, like it does with some people.

## Travelers' warnings

1–20 of **468**

### Maggot Manor

Hotel photos | Location | Symptoms | Details

**#1** of 8 vacation horrors

○○○ 376 reviews

" *got under my skin* " *August 30, 2010*

We had a shocking surprise at this Mexican manor. An ugly-looking botfly laid its eggs on my partner's skin. It turns out that the warmth of his skin caused the eggs to hatch. The larvae then burrowed under his skin and grew into plump maggots. He noticed the painful lumps when we got home. A doctor managed to pull out the hooked maggots using forceps.

« 1 2 ... 25 »

## Baghdad Bel Air

Visitors to this hotel warn of the peril posed by tiny bloodsucking sand flies in the Iraqi capital and other hot, sandy places. Evidently these little pests carry a horrid protozoan parasite called *Leishmania*. This produces unpleasant skin ulcers on exposed body parts, such as the face, arms, and legs.

## Travelers' choice awards

## More nasties!

1. Malaria menace in the Tropics
2. Tick trouble in the Northern Hemisphere
3. Beaver fever in North America
4. Burrowing hookworms in warm places
5. Traveler's diarrhea everywhere

## FREE PEST GUIDE

Get the best tips to avoid horrible vacation horrors!

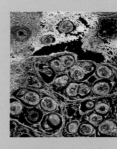

**Download PDF**

## Featured traveler video

0:45/2:01

Submitted by: ihatebugs55

### Kissing Bug Lodge

I filmed this on my boyfriend's cell phone when we were backpacking in Chile. One night he felt a bite, and we saw this kissing bug sucking blood through his skin and defecating. Its feces contain protozoan parasites. If you scratch them into your blood—thankfully, he didn't—they can give you Chagas' disease, which affects the heart and digestive system.

## Worms Retreat

**#2** of 8 vacation horrors

○○○ 376 reviews

" *avoid the lakes* "    August 9, 2010

If you visit out-of-the-way tropical destinations, avoid lakes and rivers. Larvae of the schistosome worm can burrow through your skin and give you schistosomiasis. The worms grow in blood vessels around your bladder or intestines, where they lay their eggs.

## Diarrhea Lake

**#3** of 8 vacation horrors

○○○ 376 reviews

" *terrible pains* "    July 30, 2010

We thought the food was good, but it ruined our trip to this West African resort. I was laid low with terrible stomach pains and bloody diarrhea. Apparently the salad was washed with water carrying a tiny protozoan that gave me amebic dysentery.

## Cyst Spa

**#4** of 8 vacation horrors

○○○ 376 reviews

" *cyst in her lung* "    July 27, 2010

This place was unhygienic, with dogs and sheep everywhere. One of us ate food tainted by dog feces. These contained tapeworm eggs that normally develop into cysts inside sheep. Our friend developed a cyst in her lung the size of a grapefruit.

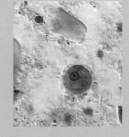

# PETRIFYING PLACES AND KILLER CULTURE

You don't have to go far to get a fright. Unnerving nightmares haunt your sleep. Evil creatures stalk you at the movies. Even your own home is packed with perilous pitfalls, waiting to turn you into a stretcher case. Still thirsting for thrills? How about a bit of bungee jumping, a mamba milking session, or a dish of deadly blowfish?

137

# WISH YOU WERE HERE?

...Perhaps not. These post-card scenes of everyday life seem harmless enough, but look more closely; unseen disasters are just waiting to happen in the most unexpected of places. These deathtraps for the unwary aren't just lurking around the corner—they're on the beach, in the kitchen, in your classroom... As the saying goes—be prepared!

## Cliffhanger

High ledges and skateboards really don't mix well. Take heed of any warning signs... if you're not riding along too fast to miss them, that is.

## The chair

Are you an avid chair tilter? Just wait until it slips and you end up on the floor with a sore head and bruised ego.

## Rip-off!

Let's hope that cat can swim! Beware of strong currents (rip currents) that rip along beneath the water's surface. They've carried this rubber ducky right out to sea.

## Rocky times

Don't be left high and dry and crabby! Waders should keep a beady eye open for the incoming tide so as not to get cut off from the shore.

## Sink or swim

As its name suggests, quicksand doesn't allow much time to react, and the more you struggle, the deeper you sink. Lie flat and try to "swim" out.

## Broken glass

Like the feel of sand between your toes? Be careful those bare tootsies don't get cut on broken glass—you never know what else might be lurking among the golden grains.

## Enjoy the trip?

Backpacks left lying in the middle of the floor are accidents just waiting to happen... and you won't need to wait long.

## That's sick

Coughs and sneezes splutter snot and germs into the air, and your desk becomes a breeding ground for colds and the flu. Use a tissue when you achoo!

## A real pain

School can be difficult enough without the added pain of a self-inflicted injury from staplers, scissors, sharpeners... Go to the back of the class.

## Take cover!

Sending books and other missiles hurtling around the classroom is an obvious danger for everyone, including the books.

## Boiling over

That pan of water could topple over the edge at any time. Hopefully, the baby won't reach up and grab the handle—it should have been turned inward.

## Bottled danger

Poisonous cleaning fluids in an open cupboard and a nearby baby is a bad combination. Babies can't read warning signs, and the bottles, to them, look just like those with soda inside.

## Washing cycle

It's a good idea to keep your eye on any pets you have in the kitchen. Henry the hamster's trip through the spin cycle will leave him feeling more than washed out.

## Disease trap

Leaving raw food uncovered on the side is an open invitation for flies and bacteria. Let's hope it won't make the family sick when they eat it.

## Killer cassava

In many parts of Africa and South America, a root vegetable called cassava is part of the staple diet. It is served as a meal accompaniment or is used ground up into a type of flour called tapioca. However, it is not a vegetable for the uninitiated; when raw, it contains the deadly toxin cyanide and must be carefully prepared and cooked if the diner wants to avoid a sticky end.

## Blowfish surprise

Known in Japan as fugu, the blowfish is the world's deadliest delicacy, causing an average of four deaths every year. Its skin and internal organs contain the powerful poison tetrodotoxin—one fish has enough to kill 30 people. In Japan, chefs train for years to serve this expensive and sought-after dish. Risky as it sounds, the most skilled chefs try to leave just the right amount of poison to give a pleasant numbing sensation on the tongue.

## Fugu Special!

Buy one get one free*

*(if you survive the first one)

## Giant bullfrog

The French may be famous for eating frogs' legs, but the people of Namibia go one step farther. The giant bullfrog, eaten whole, is considered a great delicacy there, even though its poisonous skin can cause kidney failure.

# DEADLY DINER

If you think you're taking your life in your own hands eating in the school cafeteria, check out this exotic cuisine. One visit to this deadly diner might be your last. On the menu are a selection of the most downright dangerous foods from around the world—some would be eaten only by accident, but others are highly prized delicacies.

## Kill or cure?

The oil made from the castor plant has been used for centuries as a folk remedy for all sorts of ailments, including burns, cuts, headaches—and even as a cure for acne. But the seed of the plant, known as the castor bean, contains ricin—one of nature's most lethal poisons. It would take only eight of the tiny beans to kill a person.

## Mmm! Mushroom meal deal

**Choose from one of the following five mouthwatering options:**

1. **Death cup**—looks just like edible species, but the clue's in the name.
2. **Fly agaric**—brightly colored, just 10 will kill a human.
3. **Galerina**—small mushroom, but packs a big toxic punch.
4. **Jack-o'-lantern**—bright orange, glows in the dark, and will cause severe stomach cramps if eaten.
5. **Deadly fiber cap**—contains high doses of muscarine, a lethal poison.

## Live octopus

Sannakji, or live octopus, is a popular dish in South Korea and Japan, but not one for the faint-hearted. The octopus is cut into pieces while still alive so that the tentacles wiggle around on the plate. Those who don't chew their food enough risk getting a sucker stuck in the back of their throat!

## Maggot cheese

For a cheese sensation, why not try the Sardinian delicacy Casu Marzu? Made from sheep's milk, the cheese is left outside for months to become riddled with insect larvae. The maggots wiggle throughout the cheese, digesting it as they go to make it runny and soft. Diners are advised to shield their eyes, as the maggots jump when disturbed! And, once eaten, they'll happily bore through your intestines, too.

# TOOLSHED TERRORS

Enter the dark zone of the toolshed at your peril. Danger lurks here for every do-it-yourself (DIY) enthusiast. In the U.S., one in four people receiving emergency treatment in the hospital is injured in a DIY accident—that's about four million people a year. Next time there's a quick-fix job to be done at home, remember this simple truth—the tools are out to get you!

## A step too far

Heard the one about the guy who was airlifted to the hospital with a plank of wood nailed to his head after falling from a ladder? It's not unusual. Ladders cause more accidents than almost any other item in the toolshed.

## Close shave

Beware—your lawn mower bites! Don't adjust the blades with the motor running or wear sandals to mow the lawn. You'll finish up minus fingers and toes. Look out for toys left lying in the grass, as they can bounce up and hit you in the face!

## Sticky ending

Glue comes in handy for different jobs around the house, but just be careful where you stick it. People end up in the hospital glued to all kinds of objects. Don't go spilling it on the toilet seat, as one man did...

## Nail power

High on the list of DIY horrors are nail guns. One careless slip and the nail is buried in your anatomy (usually your hand or foot) instead of the wall or floor. One man in California had six nails removed from his skull after a nail-gun accident, but he survived!

## Power play

Electrocution by drilling into electric cables, leaks from puncturing water pipes, and eye injuries as a result of using a grinder without safety glasses... The catalog of power-tool disasters goes on and on. There's one simple solution. Just turn the machine off!

## Cutting edge

From handsaws to chain saws, these tools demand respect. Most chain-saw injuries are to the legs and knees, as a result of slipping, dropping, or losing control of a running chain saw. The average chain-saw injury requires 110 stitches. Ouch!

## Fire starter

You're up in the attic using a blowtorch to burn off old paint, but the next thing you know, the whole roof is on fire and several fire engines are screeching to a halt in the street outside. It's a bit of a blow, really.

## Unhelping hand

Don't use a screwdriver to get the lid off the paint can. If it slips, you'll give yourself an injury. Now, where did you leave that hammer? It's on top of the stepladder, so climb with caution. The vast majority of DIY accidents are caused by careless slips with hand-held tools, including hammers, screwdrivers, knives, and scalpels. Remember, tools rule.

## First aid

A first-aid kit is an absolute essential in the toolshed. Heading the list of common DIY injuries are cuts to the hands and fingers, followed by specks of dust or paint in the eye. A surprising number of people push parts of their body through glass windows or doors... painful!

## In for the chop

To all of those woodcutters out there— wear heavy boots when chopping logs and make sure the head of your ax is firmly attached to the shaft before taking aim. Otherwise, you'll be getting axed, too.

# DEATH BY IDIOCY

Life is full of hidden dangers, and accidents are just waiting to happen. Despite this, some people go through life blissfully unaware of the stupidity of their own actions. This award ceremony salutes some of the truly idiotic ways in which people have brought an abrupt end to their lives. Read it and weep!

## What a pane!

This award goes to the gentleman who threw himself against the window of his 24th-floor office in an attempt to prove to a group of visitors that the glass was unbreakable. On his second attempt, he smashed through the glass and plunged to his death.

## It takes two...

Congratulations to the impatient driver who drove around the gates of a railroad crossing in a bid to beat an approaching train. He hit an oncoming car head-on because the driver coming the other way had the same idea! The train sped by unharmed.

## Snakebite

The American dream ended for one California man who picked an argument with a rattlesnake. When the man stuck his tongue out at the snake, the riled reptile retaliated by sinking its fangs into the offending item. The poor guy's tongue and throat swelled and he choked to death.

## That floored him

A bungee jumper carefully measured his bungee cords so that they would stop his fall a few feet (meters) short of the ground. Unfortunately, he overlooked the fact that the cords were made of elastic. When the man jumped, the bungee cords stretched and he hit the floor headfirst.

## Up, up, and away
A Brazilian Catholic priest attached 1,000 helium-filled balloons to a chair and launched himself skyward. His goal was to raise money for his parish work, but the weather was not on his side—strong winds blew him off course and he drifted out to sea. He was never seen again.

## Cock-a-doodle-doo!
Here's one from the history books: One cold winter's day in 1626, forward-thinking English scientist Sir Francis Bacon decided to see if he could preserve a chicken by stuffing it with snow. He caught a cold and died of pneumonia a week later.

## Wrong number
This one is dedicated to the man who was woken by a ringing telephone next to his bed. He reached out his hand to answer it, but grabbed his gun instead by accident. As he put the gun to his ear to speak, he shot himself through the head.

## Shocking story
Annoyed by the molehills spoiling his lawn, a man drove metal stakes into the ground and connected them to a high-voltage power cable. The next day, he walked onto the lawn to see if he had succeeded in frying the moles and ended up electrocuting himself.

# KILLER CAREERS

Does the idea of a desk job make you yawn? Are you looking for daring challenges rather than a boring nine-to-five? Then career through our assault course and some of the most dangerous jobs in the world. All of them carry a high risk of injury and accidental death—so hold on tight to your hardhats!

**START**

## Logger

Watch you don't slip with that chain saw, and look out for falling trees and branches! Logging (cutting down forests) is high on the list of killer careers. Good choice if you love the great outdoors, but keep a first-aid kit close at hand.

## Bomb-disposal expert

This obstacle calls for a bomb-disposal expert. They are trained to make safe any explosive device, be it an IED (roadside bomb), unexploded World War II bomb, land mine, or car bomb. This job requires patience, skill, and mega amounts of courage.

## Deep-sea diver

Your next stop is the bottom of the sea. Deep-sea divers work in dark, murky waters searching for oil and gas or repairing damaged pipelines. It's tough, dangerous work—but don't surface too quickly. Bubbles can form in the blood in a potentially lethal condition called "the bends."

## Venom milker

First, catch a poisonous snake. Next, rub its venom gland until it shoots venom from its fangs into a jar. Remember to keep some antivenin at hand—the chances of being bitten during venom milking are high. Fang-tastic work if you can get it!

## Power-line technician

Calling all live wires out there—installing and repairing high-voltage power lines is electrifying work (sometimes literally). Be prepared to work in blizzard and storm conditions—shockproof nerves and a head for heights are a must.

## Crab fisher

According to U.S. government figures, fishing for king crabs off the coast of Alaska is statistically the most dangerous job in the world. With waves as big as houses coming at you, one slip and you're a goner—no one can survive in the freezing waters.

## Miner

Venturing deep under the ground to mine for coal, gold, diamonds, or other minerals is full of dangers. Air is in short supply, and if a rock collapse or gas explosion occurs without warning, you'll be trapped. Not a career for the claustrophobic!

## Safari ranger

Those big cats don't look so friendly. Neither do angry rhinos and snap-happy crocs, not to mention armed ivory poachers. You need to keep your wits and survival skills about you as a safari ranger.

## Smoke jumper

A wildfire is spreading fast. How to tackle it before it takes hold? Send in the smoke jumpers! These firefighters parachute into remote areas to put out forest fires. Holy smoke—what if the jump goes wrong?

## Construction worker

Falls from ladders, accidents with machinery, injuries from collapsing scaffolding—construction can be a deadly business. Imagine plunging more than 40 stories from a skyscraper… It has happened.

FINISH

## FREEDIVING

Take a deep breath and hold it for up to eight minutes—or longer, if you fill your lungs with pure oxygen first. Freediving is underwater diving without any breathing apparatus and is the closest you will get to swimming like a fish. Some freedivers descend to mind-blowing depths of 328 ft (100 m) or more.

## BUNGEE JUMPING

Launch yourself into empty space with only an elastic cord attached to your feet and wait for the rebound. Crazy or what? The first loony leapers were Pacific Islanders who jumped from cliffs with liana vines tied to their ankles. Today, bungee jumpers fling themselves from tall structures all over the world.

## DIRTBOARDING

Too warm for snowboarding? Why not try your hand (or should that be foot?) at dirtboarding? A dirtboard, which is also called a mountainboard, is mounted on four wheels and can be ridden on any surface—grass, dirt track, concrete... You name it. You can even use it for land kitesurfing.

## SNOWBOARDING

Snooow-exciting... There's nothing to beat the adrenaline rush of "surfing" the fresh powder as you slide and float down a mountainside on your board—a thrilling combination of skateboarding, surfing, and skiing. Best not to take any foolish risks, though—avalanches and giant tumbles can prove fatal.

## BMX FREESTYLE

Looks so easy, but BMX (bicycle motocross) freestyle requires enormous strength and skill. Riders continually push themselves to and the limit as they race up a vertical halfpipe (ramp) to perform leaps and stunts in the air or show off amazing feats of balance and dexterity riding on the flat. On your bike!

## PARCOUR

Leap walls, scale buildings, run across rooftops, and jump from obstacle to obstacle with only the strength of your body to help you. This extreme physical sport, which originated in France, is also known as parcour, PK, and urban freeflow. Whatever the label, it's a cheap way for fast-moving city dwellers to travel—the only fuel used is adrenaline.

## STREET LUGE

Looking to get downhill fast? Lie back on your luge board and let gravity do the rest. Street luge started among skateboarders back in the 1970s. Experienced lugers may reach speeds of up to 80 mph (128 km/h) as they hurtle down the course, their bodies suspended a mere 2 in (5 cm) above the ground. Awesome!

## MOTOCROSS

Encounter thrills and spills galore in the supercharged world of motocross. These riders have to be mega fit as they struggle to keep control of their heavy all-terrain motorcycles. They can race at top-speed over off-road dirt tracks or perform death-defying backflips, leaps, and acrobatic stunts on fiendishly designed courses. Turn up the throttle—vroooom!

## BIG WAVE SURFING

Ride giant killer waves as tall as houses on surfboards known as "guns" or "rhino chasers." The brute force of a breaking wave can send you spinning way down below the surface with only seconds to get out before the next wave hits you. Stay under the water for three waves and you're most likely waving goodbye forever.

## WINGSUIT FLYING

Try free-falling from a plane or helicopter wearing a birdman suit with fabric wings under the legs. The fabric between the arms and legs spreads out to give your body lift, and you are free to glide high with the eagles. Just remember to release your parachute to descend gently back to Earth. Talk about a bird's-eye view!

# FEEL THE BURN

Each and every one of these extreme sports is guaranteed to deliver that moment of danger and pure terror when the adrenaline rush kicks in, stress levels soar, the muscles go into overdrive. Warning: these activities are not for the faint-hearted. Stay streetwise and always follow the safety rules.

## Channel 1: The great escape artist

A padlocked steel box is lowered into a river. Inside, wrapped in chains, is Harry Houdini, the granddaddy of stuntmen back in the early 1900s. To the amazement of the crowd, he frees himself in three minutes and swims up to the surface.

## Channel 2: Hang on a minute

Don't miss your chance to see one of the classic movie stunts of all time when silent movie star Harold Lloyd hangs onto the hands of a clock high up above a city street in the 1923 movie *Safety Last!*. The mild-mannered actor designed and performed all of his own stunts.

STV 1

## Channel 3: The jumper

In memory of Alain Prieur (07/04/1949–11/08/2007), stuntman supreme, who fearlessly leaped 16 buses on his motorcycle and jumped from 13,123 ft (4,000 m) without a parachute. Tragically, he died when his chute failed as he jumped between two gliders flying one under the other.

## Channel 4: Long-distance leaper

Relive the moment that Ke Shou Liang makes a stupendous leap in his Mitsubishi sports car across the Hukou waterfall on China's Yellow River in 1997. This movie actor and stuntman first hit the headlines after jumping his motorcycle over the Great Wall of China in 1992.

STV 4

## Channel 5: Jetman

Is it a bird? Is it a plane? No, it's Yves Rossy, the Swiss pilot who flies with a jet-powered fixed wing on his back at speeds of up to 186 mph (299 km/h). Watch in disbelief as he crosses the English Channel in under 10 minutes on September 26, 2008.

## Channel 6: Don't look down

You need a head for heights just to look at Eskil Ronningsbakken riding a bike upside down on a wire suspended 3,280 ft (1,000 m) above a Norwegian fjord! The extreme balancing acts of this fearless daredevil appear to defy the laws of gravity.

STV 7

## Channel 7: Urban climber

Who's that tapping on the window? Why, it's Alain Robert, the French Spiderman with a passion for scaling skyscrapers. Cheered on by office workers more used to the sight of pigeons than headstrong climbers, he races to the top of the world's tallest towers.

STV 2

STV 3

STV 5

STV 6

# DANCING WITH DEATH

All of our channels on Stunt TV are dedicated to the world's greatest stuntmen and their death-defying feats of sheer lunacy. Gasp at the amazing bravado of these super-crazy heroes as they hang by their fingertips from skyscrapers with ice-cold calm or leap fearlessly across yawning gorges.

## STUNT TV

# Philippe Petit

## the skywalker of New York

SIX YEARS LATER...

LOOK, THE TOWERS ARE ALMOST FINISHED. THEY ARE 110 STORIES HIGH.

THEY'RE BEAUTIFUL. NOW IT'S TIME TO MAKE MY WALK.

YOU'RE INSANE!

AS A TEENAGER, PHILIPPE PETIT WORKED AS A STREET JUGGLER AND HIGH-WIRE WALKER IN PARIS. ONE DAY, HE WENT TO THE DENTIST WITH A TOOTHACHE. THAT'S WHEN HIS CRAZY DREAM WAS BORN.

PHILIPPE SPENT THE NEXT SIX YEARS PERFECTING HIS SKILLS AS A HIGH-WIRE WALKER. SHORTLY BEFORE THE TWIN TOWERS WERE DUE TO OPEN, HE TRAVELED TO NEW YORK CITY.

TO THE ROOF

FALSE I.D.

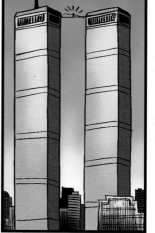

ON THE AFTERNOON OF AUGUST 6, 1974, PHILIPPE AND HIS TEAM SMUGGLED THE WIRE INTO THE WORLD TRADE CENTER. THEY TOOK THE ELEVATOR TO THE 104TH FLOOR AND THEN CLIMBED TO THE ROOF.

OVERNIGHT, THEY RIGGED UP THE WIRE BETWEEN THE TOWERS. AS A MISTY DAWN BROKE OVER MANHATTAN, PHILIPPE STEPPED OUT ONTO THE THIN STEEL CABLE SUSPENDED 1,312 FT (400 M) ABOVE THE GROUND.

WITH STEELY CONCENTRATION, PHILIPPE WALKED THE LENGTH OF THE WIRE FROM ONE BUILDING TO THE OTHER AND THEN TURNED AROUND AND WALKED BACK AGAIN.

WHAT'S THAT GUY DOING UP THERE?

HE HASN'T GOT A SAFETY HARNESS!

HE'S GONNA FALL, HE'S GONNA FALL!

I CAN'T BEAR TO WATCH!

HEY, BUD! COME BACK IN!

PHILIPPE, THEY'RE SENDING A HELICOPTER FOR YOU. GET OFF NOW—IT'S TOO RISKY.

POUF!

ZZZZZZZ

IN THE STREETS BELOW, NEW YORKERS ON THEIR WAY TO WORK GAZED UP IN ASTONISHMENT. THEY COULD NOT BELIEVE THEIR EYES.

MEANWHILE, POLICE OFFICERS APPEARED ON THE ROOF. ON SEEING THEM, PHILIPPE PERFORMED A LITTLE DANCE...

...AT ONE POINT, HE EVEN LAY DOWN ON THE WIRE.

HEY, GUYS, DON'T PUSH. ARE YOU TRYING TO KILL ME?

PHILIPPE CAME OFF THE WIRE ONLY WHEN IT STARTED TO RAIN. HE WAS IMMEDIATELY GRABBED BY THE POLICE.

FIVE DAYS LATER...

THE CHARGES ARE DROPPED.

BUT YOU MUST GIVE A STREET SHOW FOR THE CHILDREN OF NEW YORK.

WHY DID YOU DO IT, PHILIPPE?

THERE IS NO WHY. WHEN I SEE THREE ORANGES, I JUGGLE. WHEN I SEE TWO TOWERS, I WALK.

DAREDEVIL PHILIPPE BECAME AN INTERNATIONAL HERO OVERNIGHT. HE HAD PULLED OFF THE ULTIMATE HIGH-WIRE STUNT.

# EVEL KNIEVEL

THE MOTORCYCLE DAREDEVIL WHO TRIED TO JUMP THE SNAKE RIVER CANYON

MOTORCYCLE DAREDEVIL EVEL KNIEVEL REGULARLY PLAYED WITH DEATH JUMPING OVER CARS, TRUCKS, AND BUSES. HE LOST COUNT OF HOW MANY BONES HE HAD BROKEN IN HIS BODY.

ARE YOU REALLY GOING TO LEAP THAT, EVEL?

YUP!

EEK! IT MUST BE THREE-QUARTERS OF A MILE ACROSS!

HE DECIDED TO JUMP THE SNAKE RIVER CANYON IN IDAHO, A FEAT THAT WOULD BE IMPOSSIBLE ON AN ORDINARY MOTORCYCLE...

HE'S SOME CRAZY DUDE.

THEY SAY IT COST MORE THAN $150,000 TO BUILD.

THE GUY'S FEARLESS!

...SO HE BUILT A ROCKET-POWERED SKYCYCLE TO GET HIM ACROSS. IT WOULD BE HIS MOST DARING STUNT EVER.

HOPE YOU MAKE IT, EVEL.

I LIKE DOING THINGS BY THE SEAT OF MY PANTS.

THE SKYCYCLE WAS LAUNCHED UP A STEEP RAMP. PREVIOUS TEST MODELS HAD FAILED TO CLEAR THE CANYON.

THERE HE GOES!

YEE-HAW!

OOOH!

AAAAH!

EVEL PRESSED THE BUTTON AND THE SKYCYCLE ROARED UP THE RAMP AT 350 MPH (563 KM/H). IT SOARED HIGH INTO THE AIR.

HE'S GOING TO CRASH.

HE'LL DROWN.

I COULD HAVE TOLD HIM WINGS ARE BETTER.

THE PARACHUTE HAD UNFURLED TOO EARLY. PUSHED BY THE WIND, THE SKYCYCLE DRIFTED BACK INTO THE CANYON DOWN TOWARD THE SWIRLING WATERS OF THE RIVER 655 FT (200 M) BELOW.

THE SKYCYCLE CAME TO REST ON THE ROCKS JUST SHORT OF THE RIVER. MIRACULOUSLY, EVEL WALKED AWAY WITH ONLY MINOR CUTS AND BRUISES.

WHAT NEXT, EVEL?

BACK TO THE BUSES.

PAY E. Knievel $6000000

EVEL EARNED $6 MILLION FROM THE STUNT. A FEW MONTHS LATER, HE BROKE HIS PELVIS AFTER JUMPING 13 BUSES IN LONDON'S WEMBLEY STADIUM AND WENT ON TO COMPLETE MANY MORE STUNTS AND BREAK MANY MORE BONES.

# ENDURANCE

Are you ready to push your body to the limits of human endurance, and beyond? These record-breaking athletes and explorers have done just that.

### Gertrude Ederle

The first woman to swim the English Channel, Ederle set her record-breaking time of 14 hours 39 minutes in 1926, earning a ticker-tape parade in her home city of New York.

### Roald Amundsen

In 1911, this Norwegian explorer skied and dogsledded his way across Antarctica to reach the South Pole just days before British explorer Robert Falcon Scott.

### Mark Allen

This American athlete is the six-time winner of the Hawaiian Ironman triathlon event. In this supreme test of fitness and endurance, competitors complete a long-distance open swim, followed by a 112-mile (180-km) bike race, and a 26-mile (49-km) marathon run. It makes you tired just thinking about it.

### Jason Lewis

Imagine circling the globe using only muscle power. That's what British adventurer Jason Lewis did. His epic 46,000-mile (74,000-km) journey around the world took him 13 years, cycling, Rollerblading, kayaking, and pedal boating. He survived malaria, a crocodile attack, and a near-fatal road accident along the way before making it home—alive, but very, very tired.

### Martin Strel

This Slovenian swimmer battled against sunburn and exhaustion to swim the length of the Amazon River—a staggering 3,375 miles (5,431 km)—facing piranhas, anacondas, alligators, and parasitic fish that burrow into human flesh.

## Yuichiro Miura

In 1970, Japanese climber Yuichiro Miura became the first person to ski a course down Mount Everest. He covered 6,600 ft (2,011 m) in two minutes and fell another 1,320 ft (402 m) before sliding to a stop. In 2008, he made it to the top again, aged 75, and says that he'll be back for his 80th birthday.

## Ellen MacArthur

British yachtswoman Ellen MacArthur set a world record in 2005 for the fastest solo nonstop voyage around the world. Her 27,000-mile (43,000-km), 71-day odyssey pitted her skills against gale-force winds and mountainous waves. In recognition of her achievement, Queen Elizabeth II made her a dame (the female equivalent of a knight) on her return to England.

## David Hempleman-Adams

This intrepid British explorer has reached the magnetic and geographic north and south poles and completed the Seven Summits "grand slam" by climbing the highest mountain on each continent. Not content with that, he set the record for the highest ascent in a hot-air balloon—32,500 ft (9,906 m).

## Thomas Dold

Tower running is the sport of racing up the staircases of skyscrapers. In 2010, German runner Thomas Dold won the annual Empire State Building Run Up for the fifth time after pounding up 86 flights (1,576 steps) in 10 minutes.

# FRENZIED FESTIVALS

Somewhere near you, a festival is happening right now. Why not join in with the madness and mayhem? From scaring devils and staging battles to messy food fights and crazy tests of courage, festivals are a great way to let off steam—and there is often a real element of danger to the organized chaos. When the festival's over, life becomes safer and duller again. Until the next time, that is.

## IVAN KUPALA

Fire-leaping festivals are held on Ivan Kupala (Saint John's Day, July 7) in Poland, Ukraine, and Russia. Participants take turns jumping over the flames because the ritual is said to cleanse the body and mind, and bring good luck. Water fights are also part of the fun, and the festivities are well attended by locals.

## GOTMAR MELA

Every year, men from two villages in Madhya Pradesh, India, line up on both sides of a river and pelt one another with stones. The idea is to stop the rival villagers from seizing the flag attached to the top of a pole in the middle of the river.

## PAMPLONA BULL RUN

For a real taste of adventure, visit Pamplona in Spain to see young bulls being run through the town to the bullring for the festival of San Fermín. If you're daring enough, race ahead of the bulls as they charge through the narrow streets. Be careful, though—if you lose your footing, you risk being gored or trampled to death.

# CHEESE-ROLLING FESTIVAL

This bizarre annual event has been held for 200 years in Gloucestershire, England. A round cheese is set rolling down a steep hill, and racers rush down after it. Most of them finish in a pile at the bottom, often with broken bones or a sore head, but the lucky winner gets to keep the cheese. Mice one!

# BATTLE OF THE ORANGES

The town of Ivrea in Italy is the setting for this juicy annual festival when the locals dress up in medieval costumes and hurl oranges at one another. They are celebrating a battle that took place in 1194 in which the entire town rose up against a wicked duke and threw beans into the street. Since then, juicy oranges have beaten beans in the throwing stakes!

# SONGKRAN WATER FIGHT

The largest water fight in the world takes place in Thailand. To celebrate Songkran (their new-year festival in April), people spray cars and passers by with hoses, water balloons, and water guns. Everyone ends up completely drenched, but as the temperature is about 104°F (40°C)—the hottest time of the year at the end of the dry season—no one really cares!

# EL COLACHO

In the Spanish village of Castrillo de Murcia, men dressed as the devil (El Colacho) jump over babies laid in rows in the street in an annual rite to safeguard the babies from evil spirits. This unusual event takes place on the religious festival of Corpus Christi and dates back to the 17th century.

# HOW TO SURVIVE A HORROR MOVIE

Danger lurks at every turn in a horror movie, and don't you wish there was some way to stop the people in them from making the same old mistakes again and again? This instruction card has been issued as part of a campaign to make horror movies a risk-free environment and to ensure that everyone gets through them unscathed to the very end.

## 1 What not to say...

"I'll be right back."

"Who's there?"

"I'll just read this ancient spell out loud."

## 2 What not to do in a strange house...

Back out of a room without checking to see who or what's behind the door.

Open a closed door or closet if you hear strange noises on the other side.

Flee up the stairs from a monster on the loose. Once at the top, your only way out is to jump!

## 3

Never set up home next to a cemetery.

## 4

Never break into a tomb or burial ground.

## 5

Never, ever answer a ringing pay phone.

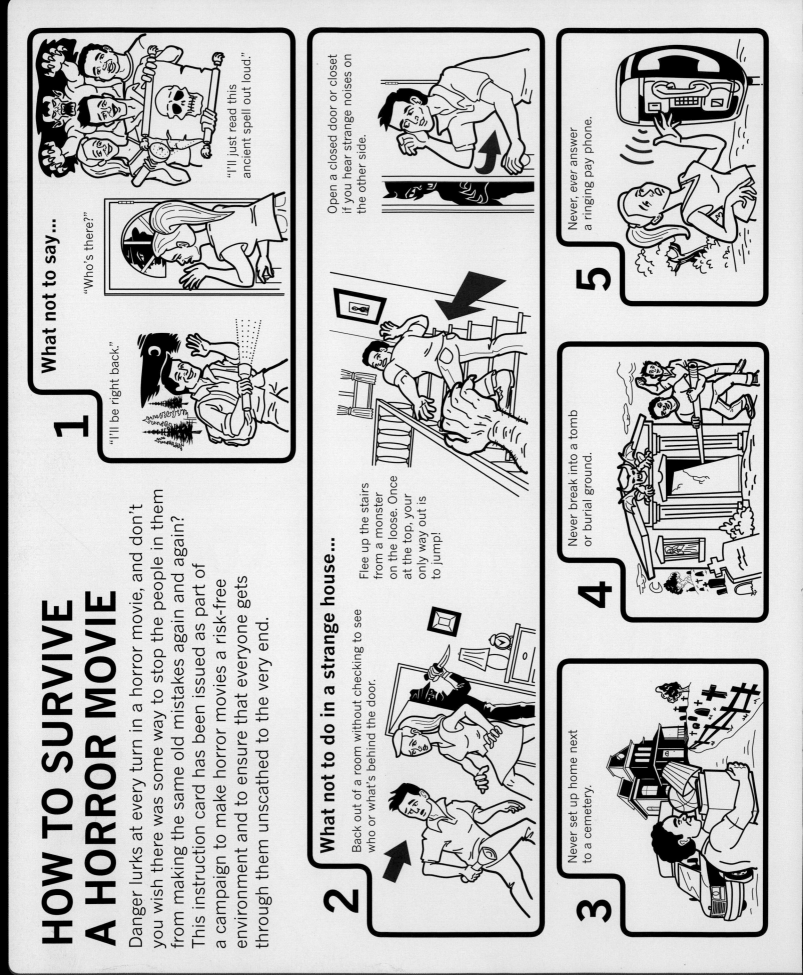

158

## What not to do when staying away from home...

**6** Be tempted to investigate a strange baying sound at night. Just assume it's a werewolf!

Plan on camping out in any woods that have a spooky name!

FOREST OF DEATH

Linger in a deserted town. The streets are empty for a reason. Take the hint and get out while you can.

**7** Be wary of anyone wearing a mask, most of all a clown's.

**8** Remember, however fast you're running away from it, the beast is always just behind you—and you're sure to fall over at least once... twice...

**9** Never watch a horror movie when you're in a horror movie.

## Banshee

You'll probably hear the banshee before you see her. This moaning spirit specializes in hanging around the house wailing when a family member is about to die. The mournful cry of a banshee can shatter glass, so have your earplugs handy.

## Grim Reaper

No one can escape the Grim Reaper. A stern figure in a hooded black cloak, he carries a scythe (an implement for cutting grass) as a sign of impending death and holds up an hourglass to show that your time is running out. You'd better quickly eat your dinner just in case.

# COME DINE WITH...

It is a dark and stormy night, and you're lost in the woods. You begin to panic when, through the trees, you see lights. Finding yourself outside a gloomy old house, you knock on the door. As it creaks open slowly, you see a table filled with food and drinks. But look at the dinner guests! Who are these creepy creatures inviting you to come dine with them? And will this be your last supper?

## Zombie

If you have a say in the seating plan, avoid sitting next to the zombie. One of the living dead, he feeds on human flesh and so is something of a picky eater. His appearance leaves a lot to be desired, and he's not much of a talker, either, as he doesn't have a mind.

## Werewolf

Take care if one of the guests starts sprouting hair. He could be a werewolf—a shape shifter who changes from a person to a wolf and back again. A silver bullet will stop him in his tracks or you could try defending yourself with your silverware if he is coming too close.

## Poltergeist

Tables and chairs are flying through the air, and you can hear pots and pans smashing to the floor in the kitchen. There is definitely a poltergeist around. These invisible spirits like to let off steam by causing a commotion. Take cover!

## Mummy

Brought back to life by an archaeologist who broke into an ancient Egyptian tomb and carelessly revived an ancient curse, the mummy is clearly very angry about something. But if you'd like some after-dinner entertainment, he's an excellent wrap artist.

## Vampire

Don't expect garlic on the menu when you dine with vampires, as they can't stand the smelly stuff. If a vampire is looking pale and interesting, he hasn't tasted human blood for a while. If you want to stop him from dining on you, be sure to have a crucifix ready.

## Ghoul

This gloomy fellow has just dropped in from the graveyard, where he likes to hang out with the local corpses and skeletons. He groans a lot, and it's never easy to cheer him up. However, he does love snacking on piles of bones, so don't bother passing him the vegetables.

## Woman in white

Feel a chill in the air? The temperature drops when ghosts like this shadowy lady are around. Ghosts can walk straight through solid walls, and they have often endured tragic deaths and seem to be searching for something... the salt and pepper perhaps?

## GET ME OUT OF HERE!

If you're unsure about how to act in a situation in the real world, your dreams can be about being trapped in an enclosed space, such as a cage or a locked room, unable to escape or scream for help. Someone who has regular dreams about this may be feeling trapped in a doomed relationship or a dead-end job.

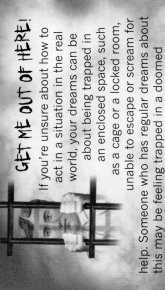

## DISASTER SCENARIO

What a disaster! You have wandered into the middle of a battle zone with explosions going off all around you. Or buildings are collapsing, or you are about to be swamped by floods, or frizzled in a fire... This is one of the most frightening types of dreams. It leaves you quivering with fright for a long time after you've woken up, unable to shake off feelings of terror and impending doom, and could reflect personal problems that you feel are raging out of control.

## FREE-FALLING

Balancing on scaffolding over a vast, empty space, you're unable to look down, but the next minute, you're falling... Running along a cliff, the ground stops suddenly and, oh no! Over you go... Nightmare! Falling is a common dream theme, reflecting inner insecurities and a feeling that there's a lack of solid grounding in your life. Thank goodness you wake up before you hit the ground!

## NO ESCAPE!

With jellylike legs and a pounding heart, you're running as fast as you can from the monster whose hot breath is bristling the hairs on the back of your neck. This nasty nightmare seems stressful in itself but could in fact be your mind's way of dealing with any stress in your waking life.

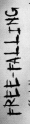

## TOOTHY TERRORS

Have you ever dreamed that your teeth are crumbling or falling out in a pile on the floor? Many people do. It could mean that you are feeling angry and clenching your teeth in your sleep or you may be worried about the way other people view you. Then again, it could just be time that you paid a visit to the dentist.

## DANGEROUS DRIVING

Behind the wheel of a car that is speeding dangerously out of control, unable to use the brakes or steering, this nightmare may drive you around the bend. And, strangely, you don't have to be a driver to experience it. Psychologists think that this nightmare is caused by anxiety about the inability to control events in real life.

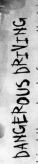

# ALL IN THE MIND

What hideous horrors are lurking in the dark depths of your subconscious? While fearsome phobias torment you during your waking hours, there are terrifying nightmares waiting to disturb your sleep. Sweet dreams...

**① FEAR OF FEATHERS**
Do feathers give you feelings of panic? Sounds like you're suffering from pteronophobia. Avoid birds!

**② FEAR OF LIGHTNING**
Officially known as astraphobia. About 50 percent of women and 10 percent of men are said to this fear of lightning and thunder can affect animals as well as people.

**③ FEAR OF SPIDERS**
have arachnophobia.

**④ FEAR OF SHADOWS**
Is that a monster? No, it's something much worse for someone with sciaphobia. It's the shadow of a monster!

**⑤ FEAR OF MIRRORS**
People who suffer from eisoptrophobia will not even hang up a mirror in case they see their own reflection.

**⑥ FEAR OF NEEDLES**
Do you shudder at the thought of giving blood? That may be because you're tryanophobic.

**⑦ FEAR OF SNAKES**
Some experts think that ophidiophobia has an evolutionary link to the fear of snakes felt by our Stone Age ancestors.

# PAST PERILS

Think things are tough today? Just take a look at some of the horrors that history inflicted on our unlucky ancestors. Ruthless rulers dealt out death and destruction, surgical skills were more barbarous than beneficial, and toenail-tearing torture was the preferred method of questioning. From dagger-toothed dinosaurs to assorted assassins, the past was a pain.

## ZONE 3—MEDIEVAL JAPAN

Test your survival skills against the NINJAS—trained assassins who use disguise and stealth to track down and silence their enemies. Specialty weapons are the shuriken (a star-shaped throwing blade) and knives. Surprise is their tactic as they scale buildings and climb trees to descend on their enemies from above.

## ZONE 4—SPANISH MAIN

In this zone, you're fighting off the PIRATES of the Caribbean. Swashbucklers such as Henry Morgan, Blackbeard, and Captain Kidd prey on Spanish ships loaded with gold bullion. Your goal is to avoid walking the plank or being keelhauled (dragged under the bottom of the ship and up the other side). Shiver me timbers!

## ZONE 2—DARK AGE EUROPE

Pit yourself against the VIKINGS. These fierce fighters from Scandinavia have sailed their dragon ships along the coasts and down the rivers of western Europe on a quest to murder, raid, and loot wherever they go. Prepare to be afraid—some of these ax-waving, battle-hardened warriors may go berserk by working themselves up into a frenzy until they feel no pain. Scary!

## ZONE 1—ROMAN EMPIRE

Your opponents are the HUNS, mounted archers who have powered their way from central Asia to destroy crops and villages and spread terror throughout the Roman Empire. Be warned—the faces of these barbarian warriors are scarred to make them look scarier. Their fearsome leader, Attila, is known as "the scourge of God." Your goal is to eliminate him. Once he is out of the way, Hun resistance will fade away.

# KILLERS ON THE LOOSE

This game is divided into seven time zones, each one controlled by a ruthless and cunning band of killers straight out of the pages of history. Your objective is to refine your defense strategies to outwit and defeat them, picking up survival points along the way. You'll need a different set of skills to complete each zone. Good luck!

1. HUN

2. VIKING

## ZONE 5—19TH-CENTURY INDIA

Try to track down the THUGGEES, followers of an Indian cult who combine robbery and ritual murder in the name of Kali, the goddess of destruction. First, they jolly up to groups of traveling merchants. Then, as night falls, they creep up silently on their companions, whip out a scarf, and throttle them. The original thugs!

## ZONE 6—OUTBACK

Prepare to do battle with the BUSHRANGERS! Hiding in the Australian outback, these runaway convicts and criminal outlaws are wanted for rustling cattle, robbing banks, and attacking travelers. Most notorious of all is Ned Kelly, who wears a suit of armor and an iron helmet and is on the run for killing three policemen.

## ZONE 7—VICTORIAN LONDON

Visit the dangerous depths of the London underworld, where GAROTERS lurk in the smoggy gloom. These heartless villains seize respectable pedestrians from behind by putting a thin wire or rope around their throat and then beating them senseless and picking their pockets. No wonder the local magazine *Punch* has advised Londoners to wear spiked metal collars for protection!

## ZONE 8—AMERICAN WILD WEST

You need to be quick on the draw to survive in this zone. There will be gun battles galore against trigger-happy gangs of WILD WEST GUNMEN. This mob is out to rob trains and banks and evade arrest by sheriffs and other law enforcers. Among the heroes and villains you'll meet are legendary outlaw Billy the Kid, train robber Jesse James, and horse-thief-turned-lawman Wyatt Earp. Get shooting!

## SELECT: KILLERS AND BATTLE ZONES

| 3. NINJA | 4. PIRATE | 5. THUGGEE | 6. BUSHRANGER | 7. GAROTER | 8. WILD WEST GUNMAN |
|---|---|---|---|---|---|

# WORLD OF PAIN

They certainly had ways of making you scream in days gone by. This torturers' catalog, issued by House of Torment, Inc., reveals bygone methods and pitiless punishments for dealing with traitors, sinners... or anyone who simply stepped out of line. Recommended revolting reading for interrogating gangs of the Inquisition and other eager torturers.

## Tongue tearers

These large iron pincers are ideal for tearing out the tongues of heretics (anyone whose religious beliefs disagree with those of the church) to permanently silence them. A simple but effective device. Recommended by Tomás de Torquemada, the head of the Spanish Inquisition, who said, "I wouldn't leave home without one."

## Iron maiden

Is there someone you'd like to put in a closet and forget about? The iron maiden may be just what you're looking for. This coffinlike box is lined with deadly spikes, so once your victim is locked inside, you can leave them to bleed to death. Beware of cheap forgeries—ours is the genuine article.

# ALL FIRED UP

Burning at the stake remains the tried and tested way of getting rid of undesirables. Our "Handy Heretic Kit" comes complete with bundles of wood, a stake, ropes, flint lighter, and a full set of instructions. Previous customers include the executioners of Joan of Arc.

# Feeling stretched?

Be the first torturer in your neck of the woods to own a rack. This cunning device stretches the body of the wretch you're tormenting until you can hear the bones crack. Even the most stubborn soul is bound to confess once the rollers start turning...

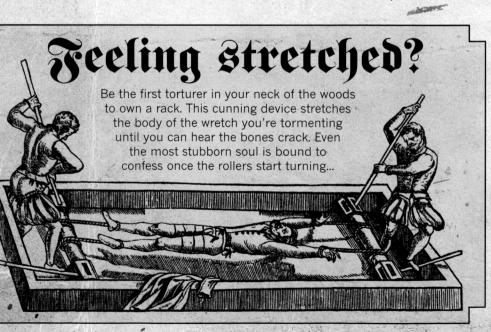

# Wheel of torture

Looking for something new in the pain department? How about the latest "Fiery Furnace" wheel of torture? Most wheel operators were satisfied with breaking their victim's arms and legs by striking them with a hammer as the body revolved around. But our new model has the novelty add-on feature of roasting the prisoner as he turns. Special offer: starter package of charcoal included.

# French guillotine

Introducing the latest idea in execution, from our Parisian friends in France. The inventor, Dr. Guillotin, claims that the French guillotine is much more humane than previous methods and will revolutionize public executions. A steel blade is raised on a rope and allowed to drop on the victim's neck, severing it from the body. We are unable to confirm reports that some heads have been seen blinking or speaking seconds after being cut off.

# Dunked!

Crabby old crones in village after village have been punished time and time again throughout history on suspicion of witchcraft. This tried-and-tested method will settle any doubts for good—sit the said person in the ducking stool, lower it into a river or pond, and hold her under the water for several minutes. If she drowns, you'll know for sure that she wasn't a witch.

# SCREWED UP

Naughty suck-a-thumbs will never suck their thumbs again if you order one of our wide range of thumbscrews. These handy devices do just what it says on the label. Ex-screw-ciating pain as the screw is turned, crushing the thumbs between the plates, is guaranteed. Just as effective on fingers and toes.

# BRAZEN BULL

Specially designed for those among you with classical tastes, we are delighted to present this well-crafted and artistic reproduction of an ancient Greek torture device. The victim is locked inside a hollow brass or bronze (brazen) bull, before a fire is lit underneath. The unlucky unfortunate is then roasted to death.

# MURDER MOST FOUL

Hello, hello, hello—what's going on at the seaside? It looks like some very dubious characters have found their way into our puppet show. Don't be fooled by these puppets, girls and boys—they are all infamous murderers. Can you help Policeman and Crocodile bring our Mr. Punch and his fiendish friends to justice? That's the way to do it!

## Mystery man

Bungling Policeman will never catch elusive Jack the Ripper, the notorious serial killer who haunted the gaslit streets of old London town in 1888. He stabbed his female victims to death, and his identity remains a mystery to this day.

## Heartless mother

In 1892, Francesca Rojas of Argentina bludgeoned her two young sons to death so that she could marry her boyfriend. Rojas confessed all after a bloody fingerprint on the door was identified as hers—a first for forensic science.

## Ax murderer

One hot summer's day in Fall River, Massachusetts, church-going Lizzie Borden brutally attacked and murdered her stepmother and father with an ax. She got away with it, though, after a jury failed to convict her in 1892.

## Doctor death

Creepy Dr. Crippen gave his wife a fatal injection, cut up her body, and buried the pieces before trying to escape to Canada with his girlfriend. The ship's captain alerted police, who were waiting for him as he stepped ashore.

## Kiss of death

In 1914, a man named Béla Kiss went off to war. Later, neighbors complained of a foul smell coming from large oil drums stored in his yard. They forced them open and found the pickled bodies of 24 women inside. Kiss had used newspaper advertisements to attract his victims.

## Double trouble

Bonnie Parker and Clyde Barrow went on a two-year robbing spree across the U.S. in the 1930s. This dastardly duo wasn't clowning around—they shot and killed 13 people, including nine police officers, before dying in a hail of bullets.

*Looking for love?*

Hard-working, unattached male would like to meet attractive young lady with a view to marriage. Must be rich. I can help you to invest your money. Interested? Send photo to BK, Hungary.

# WEAPONS OF WAR

Ever since our Stone Age ancestors first bashed one another over the heads with flint clubs, the battlefield has been a place of extreme danger. With the passage of time, the weapons used have become more and more powerful and more and more lethal. But with these weapons of mass play time, war has been waged in the sandpit; who's the king of the castle here?

## Chariot

In about 1500 BCE, the ancient Egyptians and Hittites fought pitched battles in light two-wheeled war chariots. Pulled by horses and highly mobile, each chariot carried a driver and an archer armed with a short bow to fire arrows down onto the enemy.

## Cannon

The invention of gunpowder by the Chinese in 900 CE transformed warfare. Cannons—heavy guns mounted on wooden carriages that fired stones and shells (explosive missiles)—were widespread in Europe from the 1400s onward, when battles became bloodier than ever.

## Musket

This gun was in use from the late 1600s until about 1850. It fired iron balls and had a bayonet (dagger) attached to the end of the barrel. Soldiers would fire their muskets in a single volley and then charge the enemy with their bayonets.

## Gladius

This short sword carried by Roman legionary soldiers was a fearsome weapon that could be used for cutting, chopping, thrusting, and stabbing at the enemy in the thick of battle. Roman soldiers also went to war armed with a heavy javelin and dagger.

## Tank

The heavily armored tank came into its own as a combat weapon during World War II (1939–1945). Equipped with tracks for all-terrain mobility and mounted with a gun in a rotating turret, its purpose was to advance forward and break through enemy lines.

## Trireme

This very fast warship was used by the ancient Greeks. It was powered by three rows of oarsmen seated on benches one above the other. A bronze-covered ram called a beak, which projected from the bow (front) of the trireme, was used to batter and sink enemy ships.

## Fighter plane

Flying was still in its infancy when warfare took to the air for the first time during World War I (1914–1918). Fighter planes were armed with machine guns, timed cleverly to fire between the propeller, and the pilots danced with death as they fought daring one-on-one battles in the sky.

## Poison gas

World War I saw the use of a horrible new weapon—poison gas. Chemicals (chlorine, phosgene, or mustard gas) that caused terrible burns and blindness were released into the enemy trenches. And if a soldier wasn't wearing a gas mask, the chemicals attacked the lungs after being breathed in.

## Mace

Medieval knights rode into battle armed with a mace. This weapon consisted of a heavy knobbed head mounted on a wooden shaft. A blow from a mace had great force and was powerful enough to smash through armor and chain mail.

## Crossbow

First used in Asia about 2,500 years ago, the hand-held crossbow was the supreme killing machine of late-medieval European warfare. It shot an iron bolt with enough force to penetrate a knight's armor at a distance of 600 ft (180 m).

# MAD MONARCHS

The pages of history are full of accounts of bloodthirsty monarchs who bullied and harassed their subjects (and their nearest and dearest) in truly horrible ways. Some of them were murderous psychopaths, while others were just crazy for power. Join these unruly rulers at the mad monarch's tea party. What do they have to say for themselves?

## NERO (37–68 CE)

I murdered two wives, tra la… And drowned my mother at sea, tra la la. Oh, what a musical emperor I am! They say I played my lyre while Rome burned—fiddlesticks! I took decisive action: I turned the Christians who started the fire into human torches to light my garden.

## CALIGULA (12–41 CE)

Many people think that I'm crazy, but what's the point of being the Roman emperor if you can't have a little fun? It was a good laugh to order live criminals to be fed to the lions and tigers in the arena. And if any of you sneak a look at my bald patch, you'll be headed the same way!

## BASIL II (958–1025)

As the Byzantine emperor, I have to constantly be on the lookout for rebels. One time, my army captured 15,000 enemy Bulgars. I ordered that 99 out of every 100 should be blinded, but the 100th should lose only one eye. That way, the half-blinded men could lead the others home. It was a sight for sore eyes.

## TIMUR THE LAME (1336–1405)

I'll be remembered as the last of the great Mongol warlords. My technique was to invade first and ask questions later. I burned whole cities to the ground, slaughtered the populations, and built giant towers out of their skulls. Not so lame after all, am I?

**QIN SHI HUANG (259–210 BCE)**

That's nothing, Nero. When some stuffy old scholars disagreed with me—me, the first emperor of China!—I buried hundreds of them alive. And see those terra-cotta soldiers over there? I have 8,000 of them guarding my tomb. Thousands of people died building it, but as long as I'm safe for all eternity, who cares?

**RANAVALONA THE CRUEL (1782–1861)**

People say that I murdered my husband to make myself queen of Madagascar. I'm not telling. But it's true that I terrorized and starved my subjects. One favorite trick was to dangle my enemies above a ravine and then cut the rope. More tea, anyone?

**VLAD THE IMPALER (1431–1476)**

Mmm, these stake sandwiches are absolutely scrumptious! As the prince of Wallachia, I'm always having to deal with my rotten enemies—thousands and thousands of them over the years. I like to impale them on wooden stakes. It's the best entertainment I know. You should try it, Ivan.

**IVAN THE TERRIBLE (1530–1584)**

My Russian subjects made me really angry, so I set my private army on them. For seven years they went on the rampage—looting, burning, killing, and torturing. They wore black, and their emblem was a dog's head and broom. Down, Fido—I'll feed you an aristocrat soon.

# MEDICAL HORRORS

Welcome to the House of Horrors, where each room contains a scene of surgical ghastliness. Before pain-numbing anesthetics arrived in the 19th century, any procedure that involved cutting into the body was painful and was carried out as rapidly as possible. Even in the 20th century, gruesome but useless procedures such as ice-pick lobotomies were still happening.

## ① Hole in the head

Need relief from a bad migraine or a feeling of depression? Then try a procedure that dates back to the Stone Age. Trepanation involves using a flint tool to make a circular hole in the skull bone that exposes the brain and allows the "demons" causing the problem to escape.

## ② Amputation

Saw at the ready, his patient strapped in place, this surgeon is poised to cut off the diseased arm. The operation will be painful, but he should be able to amputate the arm in under a minute. If blood loss isn't great, and the wound doesn't become infected, his patient may survive.

## ③ New teeth

The man in the chair has horrible tooth decay, the result of eating refined sugar, a new product in the 18th century. His dentist removes rotten teeth and replaces them with "new" ones taken from executed criminals or dead paupers. These transplants won't last and may also carry disease.

## ④ Bloodletting

This unfortunate woman is being bled by a surgeon. Why? It was once believed that certain ailments were the result of having an "excess" of blood in the body. The remedy was bloodletting—cutting into a vein with a sharp knife and allowing the "excess" to flow out.

## ⑥ Burn and seal

Casualties of war often have hideous injuries. In older times, battlefield surgeons would seal wounds with boiling oil to stop bleeding. This surgeon is using a more modern method—red-hot irons—to seal a wound. You may hear some sizzling!

## ⑤ Gallstone removal

This patient has a hard stone in his gallbladder causing unbearable pain. Let's hope his doctor has the skill of 18th-century surgeon William Cheselden. This speedy operator used a sharp curved knife and could cut into the gallbladder and remove a stone in only 45 seconds.

## ⑦ Ice-pick lobotomy

Dating from the 1930s, this gruesome procedure, called a lobotomy, was used for treating mental illness. The surgeon is about to hammer an ice pick through the back of the patient's eye socket and into his brain in the hope that it will change his behavior. It's more likely to drive him insane!

# KILLER CURES

The swindlers who peddled fake medicines to make money from the sick were known as "quacks." Although their cures didn't necessarily kill people, remedies supplied by these quacks could be dangerous and leave the patients even worse off. Other tonics and treatments were so useless that they did nothing at all. On offer here are some examples of toxic therapies and ridiculous remedies.

## Toad treatment

When the bubonic plague killed millions in Europe during the 14th century, all kinds of weird remedies were tried, unsuccessfully, to save lives. They included pressing dried-out toads to the boils caused by the disease to "suck out infected pus," as well as drinking a mix of eggshells and molasses.

## No more pain

Opium is a drug extracted from the poppy flower. Opium dissolved in alcohol (and called laudanum) was very popular in the Victorian era as a painkiller or sleeping pill. It took awhile for people to realize that it was dangerously addictive.

## Mercury menace

In the age of "heroic medicine," from 1780 to 1850, many aggressive but harmful treatments were used by doctors. One of these was calomel (mercury chloride), which was taken to encourage patients to "release impurities." Sadly, it also made them lose their hair and teeth, develop ulcers, and even die.

## Spot the mistake

Joshua "Spot" Ward was an 18th-century quack who invented remedies called "Ward's Pill" and "Ward's Drop" that made him rich. Made with various poisonous substances, Ward's harmful remedies caused violent sweating as the body tried to expel the toxic ingredients.

## Smoke gets in your...

The supposed stimulant effect of tobacco smoke was used for an unusual purpose during the 18th century. Using special bellows, doctors blew smoke into the rectums of people who were apparently dead from drowning. It was thought to revive them.

## Hot stuff!

Doctors of the 18th and 19th centuries believed that if inflammation inside the body was causing a disease, making the skin inflamed would "remove the disease below." Techniques used to inflame the body included bandaging burning substances to the skin to produce open sores or blisters.

## Secret recipe

In the 10th century, English quack Joanna Stephens became wealthy by concocting a potion to dissolve gallstones. It contained snails, eggshells, herbs, and soap and was completely useless. Yet the British government paid Stephens a large sum of money to reveal her secret recipe.

## Kill or cure?

In the early 20th century, radioactive substances, now known to be dangerous, were regarded as a novelty. Some quacks even sold radioactive cures. Most notorious of these was Radithor, which caused the death of at least one person from radiation poisoning.

# THE MOST DANGEROUS JOBS IN HISTORY

The poor folks in this bus line have some of the worst jobs in history. They'll be shot at, exposed to hideous diseases, and they will generally risk life, limb, and a sore behind in order to earn a buck. So if you don't want a job where you're likely to die before you punch out, don't even think about getting onboard with these sorry souls.

BUS STOP

## Arming squire

Ever dreamed of becoming a knight? To get your foot in the door, you first need to risk your neck on the battlefield as a knight's squire. Without so much as a helmet yourself, your role is to rearm your knightly master. And when the fighting's over, guess who has to clean up the mess...?

## Searcher of the dead

First in line, an old woman of plague-riddled 17th-century Europe was the favored candidate for the job of "dead body inspector." A sharp eye to spot plague victims was essential. Not a job with long-term prospects, as the deadly disease is highly contagious.

## Lancaster gunner

Cramped in a tiny turret, at the rear of a lightly armored plane that is showered with bullets night after night, the gunner of a Lancaster Bomber plane had a tough job just staying alive. The life expectancy of a rear gunner on this British World War II plane was said to be only five missions.

## Roman gladiator

Although some ancient Roman gladiators may have been famous, most were poor slaves who were trained to fight in front of bloodthirsty crowds. If they lost their bouts in the arena but didn't die of their wounds, they could be killed by an executioner.

## Whipping boy

Back in Tudor England, royal children could be punished only by the king. Tutors who needed to discipline their charges had to punish the royal child's companion instead, whose job it was to take all of the beatings to save the royal backside. It was a real pain in the bum.

## Lady in waiting

In medieval India, a princess's lady in waiting had a comfortable life. Until her mistress's husband died, that is. Then, his wife and all of their servants were thrown onto the funeral pyre to keep him company in the afterlife. No need to worry about references...

## Royal food taster

You may have "royal" in your title, but accepting the job of royal food taster is nothing but a royal blunder. Employed throughout history by monarchs, the job entailed sampling food in case it had been laced with poison by a would-be assassin. Take this job, and each meal could be your last.

## Petardier's assistant

During the English Civil War, small bombs called petards were used to blow open walls and fortifications. But first, someone had to attach them to the walls and fortifications. Step up the plucky petardier's assistant, ready to dodge flying bullets to get the job done... if the bombs didn't blow him up first.

# THE MOST DANGEROUS AGE?

Living is an age-old risky business. Disease, famine, war, fire, floods, or earthquakes may cut lives short in a heartbeat. But, around the world, life expectancy has slowly risen over the centuries, although at different paces in different places. Trace the human lifeline, beat by perilous beat, on this cardiogram of existence and follow the changing threats to human survival throughout the different periods of history.

## Classical Age
## 600 BCE–400 CE

War just kept getting tougher and meaner. The Greeks were always fighting one another when not fighting the Persians, while the Romans would pick a fight with anyone. Galley oarsmen and gladiators were unlikely to live long in their line of work. On the plus side, the Greeks were good at medicine and the Romans believed in sanitation.

## Stone Age
## 150,000–7000 BCE

Life was tough during the Ice Age. Living in caves and hunting wild animals with spears and arrows meant that most people died before they were 25. As Earth warmed up, hunter-gatherers were able to find more animals and plants to eat. In time, life became easier and people lived longer.

## Early civilizations
## 4000–1200 BCE

Times were good for kings and priests at the top but difficult for everyone else, such as farmers, soldiers, and common laborers. Diseases like smallpox and measles spread as they were passed to humans from newly domesticated livestock. The chances of being killed in battle, slain as a prisoner, or sacrificed upon the death of a ruler were scarily high.

## Age of exploration
## 1500–1750

Europeans spread guns and disease around the world as they built up trading empires and colonies. Enslaving "uncivilized" native peoples, they then began a deadly trade in human lives, deporting African slaves to the New World. Within the European homelands, too, thousands more were killed in the wars of religion that swept across the continent as Catholics and Protestants battled it out for supremacy.

## 20th century

Although life expectancy in the western world exceeded 75 years by the year 2000, in the poorest countries it was only about 40 years. More people died in war than in any other century, with 20 million deaths in World War I and 55 million in World War II alone. Millions more died in terrible famines and disease epidemics, such as the flu and AIDS.

## Industrial Age
## 1750–1900

Better medical knowledge and improved sanitation meant that people could expect to live longer and longer... but only if they were rich. For industrial workers living in crowded, polluted cities, life expectancy was much lower. More than 500,000 Americans died in the terrible slaughter of the American Civil War between 1861 and 1865.

## Middle Ages
## 400–1500 CE

With barbarian invaders, Viking raiders, Mongol horsemen, castle sieges, and frequent famines, the Middle Ages were a dangerous time for kings and serfs alike. The worst event of all was the Black Death (bubonic plague), which wiped out one third of Europe's population in the 1340s.

# BLASTS FROM THE PAST

What's with this scene of rampage and riot? These skin-slashing, bone-crushing prehistoric animals are among the biggest and most dangerous creatures that have ever lived on Earth... Run for your life!

## GIGANOTOSAURUS ▶

The world's largest predatory dinosaur, this monster was an impressive 45 ft (13.7 m) long from head to tail, but had a brain the size of a banana. It lived 100–95 million years ago and killed its prey (smaller dinosaurs) by slashing their flesh with its long daggerlike teeth.

## SABER-TOOTHED TIGER ▶

This snarling cat is a comparative child—it died out at the end of the last ice age, about 11,000 years ago. With its powerful jaw and long, curved upper canine teeth, it was a deadly killing machine that ambushed its unsuspecting prey.

## ▼ GIANT SEA SCORPION

The biggest bug of history lived on Earth 400 million years ago and was an amazing 8.2 ft (2.5 m) long—the size of a large crocodile. Not something you'd want to meet on an afternoon stroll.

## ▲ TITANOBOA

Frightened of snakes? You soon will be if this giant boa constrictor is after you. Measuring 40–50 ft (12–15 m), this hissing reptile was twice as long as the anaconda—the longest snake in the world today—and lived in the South American rainforests about 60 million years ago.

## PREDATOR X ▶

Look out! With a bite 10 times stronger than any animal alive today, this pliosaur (marine reptile) will make mincemeat of your motorboat. The most fearsome monster ever to swim the seas, it ruled the Jurassic oceans about 147 million years ago.

## ▼ MEGALODON

More than twice as long as the great white shark—its closest living relative—*Megalodon* was a massive 40 ft (12 m) long. It could open its toothy jaws 7 ft (2 m) wide—enough to gobble up a Jet Skier in a single gulp.

## DIATRYMA ▶

A giant flightless bird that lived 56–33 million years ago, *Diatryma* used its clawed feet to bring down small mammals. It then finished them off with a bone-crushing bite to the back of the neck from its large parrotlike beak. Pretty Polly!

## ◀ GIANT RODENT

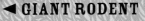

Between four and two million years ago, a rodent as large as a buffalo grazed the vegetation of South America. Its skull alone was more then 20 in (50 cm) long. Known as *Josephoartigasia monesi*, this giant guinea pig weighed a heavy, person-squashing ton (tonne).

## ◀ GODZILLA

This terrifying monster from the deep is an ancestor of the crocodile. It had a head like a dinosaur's, and its body ended in a fishlike tail. No wonder they call it Godzilla! Officially named *Dakosaurus andiniensis*, it thrived 135 million years ago.

# Index

# Acknowledgments

**DK WOULD LIKE TO THANK:**
Gail Armstrong, Army of Trolls, Ben the illustrator, Mick Brownfield, Seb Burnett, Kat Cameron, Rich Cando, Karen Cheung, Mike Dolan, Hunt Emerson, Lee Hasler, Matt Herring, Matt Johnstone, Toby Leigh, Ellen Lindner, Mark Longworth, John McCrea, Jonny Mendelsson, Peter Minister, Al Murphy, Neal Murren, Jason Pickersgill, Pokedstudio, Matthew Robson, Piers Sanford, Serge Seidlitz, Will Sweeney, and Mark Taplin for illustrations. www.darwinawards.com for reference material for "Death by idiocy." Stephanie Pliakas for proofreading. Jackie Brind for preparing the index. Stephanie Pliakas and John Searcy for Americanization.

The publisher would like to thank the following for their kind permission to reproduce their photographs:

(Key: a-above; b-below/bottom; c-center; f-far; l-left; r-right; t-top)

**Endpaper images: NHPA / Photoshot**: Daniel Heuclin (bird). **Corbis**: Tom Grill (beaker). **Corbis**: Hal Beral (cuttlefish). **iStockphoto.com**: diane39 (toy soldier with trumpet). **iStockphoto.com**: MrPlumo (mountain warning icons). **Alamy**: anthony ling (puppets). **Getty Images**: Popperfoto (Bonnie Parker). **Getty Images**: (Clyde Barrow). **iStockphoto.com**: Fitzer (frames). **iStockphoto.com**: messenjah (toy soldier crawling). **Getty Images**: S Lowry / Univ Ulster (SEM tuberculosis). **Science Photo Library**: Hybrid Medical Animations ( AIDS virus). **Getty Images**: (Dr Crippen). **Alamy**: INTERFOTO (doctor's outfit). **Corbis**: Lawrence Manning (toy stethoscope). **iStockphoto.com**: jaroon (men in chemical suits). **Corbis**: Creativ Studio Heinemann / Westend61 (salamander). **Getty Images**: CSA Plastock (orange toy soldier). **iStockphoto.com**: Antagain (wasp side view). **Getty Images**: Schleichkorn (hantavirus). **iStockphoto.com**: ODV (dynamite). **Getty Images**: (toad). **Getty Images**: Science VU / CDC (West Nile virus). **Corbis**: Wave (monarch butterfly, side view). **Corbis**: Randy M Ury (monarch butterflies). **Getty Images**: Renaud Visage (wasp in flight). **iStockphoto.com**: grimgram. **iStockphoto.com**: YawningDog (medicine bottle). **Getty Images**: Retrofile (woman with hands over mouth). **Getty Images**: SuperStock (frightened woman).

**2-3 iStockphoto.com**: pialhovik. **4-5 iStockphoto.com**: pialhovik. **6 iStockphoto.com**: jamesbenet. **6-7 iStockphoto.com**: pialhovik. **18 Alamy Images**: Arco Images GmbH. **Getty Images**: Peter Lilja (c). **18-19 Getty Images**: Ian Logan (t). **19 Alamy Images**: Bob Gibbons. **Getty Images**: Don Farrall (bl); Nick Gordon (br); GK Hart / Vicky Hart (cb). **20 Corbis**: CDC / PHIL (bl); Dennis Kunkel Microscropy, Inc / Visuals Unlimited (tr); Dr David Phillips / Visuals Unlimited (br); Visuals Unlimited (tl). **20-21 iStockphoto.com**: Paha_L (bc). **21 Alamy Images**: Peter Arnold, Inc (clb). **Getty Images**: Retrofile (cl); SuperStock (r). **naturepl.com**: Pete Oxford (tr). **22-23 Getty Images**: Panoramic Images. **24 Corbis**: Hal Beral (bl); Stephen Frink (cb); Tom Grill (beaker). **NHPA / Photoshot**: Daniel Heuclin (tc). **24-25 Corbis**: Image Source (tc); Sebastian Pfuetze. **Getty Images**: (bc). **25 Corbis**: Creativ Studio Heinemann / Westend61 (bc); Tom Grill (tr); Randy M Ury (tl/monarch butterfly); Wave (t/monarch butterfly, side view). **34 iStockphoto.com**: JulienGrondin. **34-35 iStockphoto.com**: pialhovik. **38 iStockphoto.com**: lissart (tr); msk.nina (ftr); Vlorika (tl) (b). **38-39 iStockphoto.com**: Jeroen de Mast (t/background). **39 Getty Images**: SSPL via Getty Images (1/c). **iStockphoto.com**: lissart (tl) (bl) (cr); msk.nina (cla) (cra) (fbl); Vlorika (tr) (br). **40-41 iStockphoto.com**: Platinus. **44 Getty Images**: Dave Bradley Photography (tl); Joel Sartore (bl). **iStockphoto.com**: Barcin (cl) (crb) (tr); StanRohrer (br). **44-45 Getty Images**: Adalberto Rios / Szalay Sexto Sol; Jean Marc Romain (b). **45 Alamy Images**: Lonely Planet Images (cra). **Corbis**: Rob Howard (bc); Jim Zuckerman (fbr). **Getty Images**: Reinhard Dirscherl / Visuals Unlimited, Inc (tl). **iStockphoto.com**: Barcin (cl) (fcra) (tr). **Science Photo Library**: Sinclair Stammers (cla). **50 Corbis**: Association Chantal Mauduit Namaste (ftl); Galen Rowell (ftr). **iStockphoto.com**: MrPlumo (tc) (bc) (bl) (br) (c) (ca) (cb) (cl) (cla) (clb) (cra) (fcra) (tr). **50-51 Getty Images**: Jupiterimages. **51 Getty Images**: AFP (cr). **iStockphoto.com**: julichka; MrPlumo (tc). **52 Getty Images**: Stockbyte (bl). **52-53 Corbis**: Dennis M Sabangan / epa (cb). **Getty Images**: InterNetwork Media (tc); Wayne Levin (bc); Tom Pfeiffer / VolcanoDiscovery (ca). **iStockphoto.com**: jeremkin. **53 Getty Images**: Steve and Donna O'Meara (br); Time & Life Pictures (tr). **54 Corbis**: George Hall (tr); James Leynse (cl). **55 Corbis**: Bettmann (tl) (b) (tr). **56 Alamy Images**: Pearlimage (tr). **Corbis**: Pascal Parrot / Sygma (cl). **Getty Images**: (tl/painting); Stephen Swintek (cr). **iStockphoto.com**: klikk (cl/frame); kryczka (tl).

**56-57 iStockphoto.com**: Juanmonino (t); paphia (wallpaper); Spiderstock (c). **57 Dreamstime.com**: Tomd (r). **Getty Images**: Andreas Kindler (cl). **iStockphoto.com**: bilberryphotography (tr); Pojbic (bc); stocksnapper (fbr). **62 Getty Images**: Colin Anderson (r); European (cb). **iStockphoto.com**: Michael Fernahl (bl/burned paper); kWaiGon (bl/smoke); manuel velasco. **62-63 Getty Images**: Arctic-Images (raindrops). **iStockphoto.com**: Grafissimo (t/frame). **63 Corbis**: Jim Reed (tl/hailstone); Peter Wilson (r). **iStockphoto.com**: Dusty Cline (bl); DNY59 (cr); hepatus (bc) (tc); Jen Johansen; Andreas Unger (tl). **Science Photo Library**: Daniel L Osborne, University of Alaska / Detlev van Ravenswaay (tc/red sprite lightning). **66 Corbis**: NASA (bl); Radius Images (cl). **Getty Images**: Andy Rouse (br). **iStockphoto.com**: UteHil (tl). **66-67 Corbis**: Bettmann. **67 Corbis**: Arctic-Images (tc); Orestis Panagiotou / epa (bl); Visuals Unlimited (tr). **Getty Images**: Georgette Douwma (br). **iStockphoto.com**: Ybmd (tl). **NASA Goddard Space Flight Center** : http://veimages.gsfc.nasa.gov (bc). **68 iStockphoto.com**: -cuba- (fbl/Coloured glossy web buttons); grimgram (fcl); k-libre (fclb/web icons); natsmith1 (c) (cr). **69 Getty Images**: Harald Sund (bc). **iStockphoto.com**: -cuba- (bl); Denzorr (tc); ensiferum (ftl); narvikk (br); TonySoh (tl); Transfuchsian (tr); yewkeo (ftr). **70 iStockphoto.com**: bubaone. **70-71 iStockphoto.com**: pialhovik. **72 Corbis**: Bettmann (cb); William G Hartenstein (cra). **Getty Images**: Time & Life Pictures (tr). **Science Photo Library**: Detlev van Ravenswaay (cr). **72-73 iStockphoto.com**: ZlatkoGuzmic. **73 Corbis**: Bettmann (fbl) (fcl). **Getty Images**: (fclb); Chad Baker (tl); Don Farrall (cla); Stuart Paton (tr); SSPL via Getty Images (ftr). **Science Photo Library**: NASA (ca). **74 Corbis**: HBSS (cl). **NASA**: (bl). **75 iStockphoto.com**: angelhell (cb/leg muscles) (tc/brain); Eraxion (ca/heart); lucato (bc/hand); mpabild (c). **80 Corbis**: Denis Scott (bc) (ca). **Getty Images**: Stocktrek RF (cr). **iStockphoto.com**: bubaone (l); lushik (bl); Mosquito (tc); rdegrie (fcl). **80-81 NASA**: JPL-caltech / University of Arizona (b). **81 Corbis**: Denis Scott (cl) (bl) (br). **Getty Images**: Antonio M Rosario (fcr); Time & Life Pictures (tc); World Perspectives (fcl). **iStockphoto.com**: Qiun (fbr). **82 Corbis**: Hello Lovely (cl); Image Source (br); Kulka (tr). **iStockphoto.com**: Ljupco (bl/hip hop artist). **82-83 Corbis. 83 Corbis**: Bloomimage (tc); Peter Frank (crb/beach); Klaus Hackenberg (cr/floodlights); Bob Jacobson (tr); Radius Images (br/deckchairs). **90 iStockphoto.com**: browndogstudios. **90-91 iStockphoto.com**: pialhovik. **92 Corbis**: Library of Congress - digital ve / Science Faction (cr). **Getty Images**: (r) (l); Time & Life Pictures (cl). **92-93 Getty Images**: Charles Hewitt. **93 Alamy Images**: INTERFOTO (tc/ Santorino Santonio). **Corbis**: Bettmann (c). **Getty Images**: (r). **iStockphoto.com**: huihuixp1 (tc/frame). **94 Corbis**: Dennis Kunkel Microscropy, Inc / Visuals Unlimited (cl/anthrax spores); National Nuclear Security Administration / Science Faction (tr/mushroom cloud); Sion Touhig (cla/dead sheep). **iStockphoto.com**: adventtr (br); arquiplay77 (tc); goktugg (tl/lined paper) (ca/Top Secret); Oehoeboeroe (tc/confidential stamp) (cr); ranplett (tr) (bl). **94-95 iStockphoto.com**: benoitb. **95 Alamy Images**: offiwent.com (fbl). **Corbis**: Handout / Reuters (tr). **iStockphoto.com**: deeAuvil (t/ folder); evrenselbaris (cl/ink splats); jpa1999 (c/open book); Kasiam (c/pen); Oehoeboeroe (tc) (cb) (cr); subjug (b/folder). **98 iStockphoto.com**: gynane (br); spxChrome (tl) (cb); wir0man (fclb). **98-99 iStockphoto.com**: lordsbaine; pederk (explosion). **99 Getty Images**: Jeffrey Hamilton (br). **iStockphoto.com**: GeofferyHoman (bc); ODV (tr); spxChrome (bl) (cla). **100 Getty Images**: S Lowry / Univ Ulster (cla); Dr F A Murphy (ca); Bob O'Connor (bl); Science VU / CDC (cra). **iStockphoto.com**: jaroon (bc) (br) (cb). **Science Photo Library**: CDC (tr). **100-101 iStockphoto.com**: Fitzer. **101 Corbis**: Sean Justice (b/rope barrier); Visuals Unlimited (tr). **Getty Images**: Clive Bromhall (clb); Bob Elsdale (tc); Bob O'Connor (bl); Schleichkorn (cr). **iStockphoto.com**: jaroon (br) (bc); pzAxe (ftl). **Science Photo Library**: London School of Hygiene & Tropical Medicine (tl); Science Source (cl). **102 Alamy Images**: ICP (tl/shop interior). **iStockphoto.com**: Geoffery Holman (br); LisaInGlasses (cr/shop sign). **102-103 Alamy Images**: Art Directors & Trip (shop window). **iStockphoto.com**: avintn (b). **103 Alamy Images**: ICP (tr/shop interior). **106-107 iStockphoto.com**: tibor5. **108 Corbis**: Library of Congress - digital ve / Science Faction (tl). **109 Corbis**: Caspar Benson (cr/ treasure chest); Fabrice Coffrini / epa (br/figures); Michael Freeman (clb); Reed Kaestner (bc); Radius Images (c/skeleton). **114 iStockphoto.com**: hunkmax. **114-115 iStockphoto.com**: pialhovik. **118 Corbis:** Dr John D Cunningham / Visuals Unlimited (fbl); Tomas Rodriguez (bc). **Science Photo Library**: BSIP Ducloux / Brisou (crb); Clouds Hill Imaging Ltd (fbr); Eye of Science (bl). **118-119 iStockphoto.com**: gmutlu. **119 Corbis**: Dr Dennis Kunkel / Visuals Unlimited (fbr); Photo Division (br); Christine Schneider (fbl); Visuals Unlimited (bl) (cr). **Science Photo Library**: E R Degginger (c). **122 Getty Images**: Charles Nesbit (3/bc/wasp); Renaud Visage (2/bc/wasp). **iStockphoto.com**: Antagain (1/bc/ wasp ) (4/bc/wasp) (5/bc/wasp) (6/bc/wasp). **124 Alamy Images**: Mary Evans Picture Library (crb); Old Paper Studios (clb). **Corbis**: Bettmann (cra). **Getty Images**: Theodore de Bry (cla). **iStockphoto.com**: tjhunt (tr) (bl) (br) (tl). **124-125 iStockphoto.com**: hanibaram. **125 Alamy Images**: Peter Treanor (cr). **iStockphoto.com**: tjhunt (t) (br) (c) (clb). **Science Photo Library**: Hybrid Medical Animations (bl); National Museum of Health and Medicine (tc). **128 Getty Images**: David Chasey (cr). **iStockphoto.com**: alashi (cb); IgorDjurovic (t); JohnnyMad (fbl); ULTRA_GENERIC (bl); WendellandCarolyn (clb) (c). **128-129 Alamy Images**: David Cole; Freshed Picked (c). **129 Getty Images**: Tom Grill (fbr). **iStockphoto.com**: EuToch (cb); WendellandCarolyn (br); windyone (bc). **132 Getty Images**: Manfred Kage (tl). **iStockphoto.com**: -cuba- (fbl) (fclb/refresh icon); k-libre (fcl/home icon) (clb/hotel icon) (tc/restaurant icon); roccomontoya (ftl); RypeArts (fcla); xiver (bc/Pointing finger). **Science Photo Library**: Eye of Science (cra); A Rider (bc). **132-133 Getty Images**: Kallista Images (background). **iStockphoto.com**: k-libre (3/Web icons set). **133 iStockphoto.com**: Pingwin (ftr/insects) (cra/volume icon); runeer (ca/icon); ThomasAmby (tl/award ribbon); xiver (ftr/pointing finger icon) (clb) (crb) (fclb). **Science Photo Library**: (tl); Herve Conge, ISM (bc); Eye of Science (br); National Cancer Institute (bl); Sinclair Stammers (ca). **136 iStockphoto.com**: 4x6 (l); apatrimonio (r). **136-137 iStockphoto.com**: pialhovik. **138-139 iStockphoto.com**: zoomstudio (t/old grunge postcard). **139 iStockphoto.com**: zoomstudio (b/old grunge postcard). **144-145 iStockphoto.com**: soberve. **148-149 Corbis**: Sandro Di Carlo Darsa / PhotoAlto. **150 Corbis**: Reuters (br). **Getty Images**: (tr); AFP (cr). **150-151 Corbis**: Annebicque Bernard / Sygma (b); Kirsty Wigglesworth / POOL / Reuters (monitors). **Getty Images**: Jorg Greuel. **151 Corbis**: Jean-Christophe Bott / epa (cl); Pascal Parrot (tr); Tim Wright (br). **Getty Images**: (tl); Barcroft Media via Getty Images (cr). **154 Corbis**: CHINA PHOTOS / Reuters (cb); James Nazz (tr/lockers) (br); Andy Rain / epa (cla). **Getty Images**: (ftl) (tc); Caspar Benson (cra); Brian Hagiwara (tr/pink and green bottles); Popperfoto (fcl); Stockbyte (tr/ orange bottles); WireImage (clb). **iStockphoto.com**: Pannonia (crb). **155 Corbis**: Stephen Hird / Reuters (cla) (bl/ lockers); James Nazz (tl/lockers). **Getty Images**: (clb); AFP (br); Jeremy Woodhouse (fbl). **iStockphoto.com**: PLAINVIEW (cr). **Miura Dolphins**: (tl); Akira Kotani (tc). **156 Corbis**: Frank Muckenheim / Westend61 (br). **Getty Images**: AFP (cra). **157 Corbis**: Image Source. **Getty Images**: (cla). **160 Alamy Images**: Photos12 (c) (tr). **Getty Images**: Headhunters (l); Geir Pettersen (ca); Kamil Vojnar (tc). **161 Alamy Images**: Photos12 (tl/head) (cr). **Corbis**: Bettmann (r). **Getty Images**: Chip Simons (cra). **The Kobal Collection**: Hammer (cla). **164 iStockphoto.com**: Denzorr (r). **164-165 iStockphoto.com**: pialhovik. **168 Alamy Images**: Paul Laing (bl); Pictorial Press Ltd (br). **Corbis**: Eric Thayer / Reuters (tl). **Getty Images**: (cr). **iStockphoto.com**: sx70 (t). **168-169 iStockphoto.com**: goktugg (splashed paper); spxChrome (folded poster background). **169 Alamy Images**: INTERFOTO (clb); Timewatch Images (cla). **Corbis**: Bettmann (tl); Chris Hellier (br). **fotolia**: AlienCat (tr). **Getty Images**: SSPL via Getty Images (bl). **170 Alamy Images**: INTERFOTO (fcl) (clb) (fbr); Ian McKinnell (cl) (crb). **Corbis**: Bettmann (cra); Lawrence Manning (fcrb/stethoscope). **Getty Images**: (fcr); Sam Chrysanthou (c). **170-171 Getty Images**:; Matt Henry Gunther (bc). **171 Alamy Images**: anthony ling (br); Ian McKinnell (tl). **Getty Images**: (cr); Burazin (fbr); Popperfoto (fcr). **172 iStockphoto.com**: messenjah (clb). **173 Getty Images**: CSA Plastock (tr). **iStockphoto.com**: diane39 (bc); matt&stustock (br); messenjah (cb); wragg (crb). **180 iStockphoto.com**: AdiGrosu (tl/stethoscope); buketbariskan (crb/snail shells); dirkr (fcra/black liquid in medicine bottle); EmiSta (ca/mouse); Floortje (cra/ bandage); kamisoka (tr/old envelope); kramer-1 (bc/label); LuisPortugal (ftr/snail) (ca/medicine bottle) (cb/three bottles); Luso (fclb/empty bottle); pjjones (tr/toad); pkline (bl); rzdeb (cra/ blood stain); sharambrosia (br/pestle & mortar); Westlight (tl/ corks). **180-181 iStockphoto.com**: PhotographerOlympus (floor); zmeel (tc/cardboard box). **181 iStockphoto.com**: Angelika (tl/ cardboard box); BP2U (crb); cloki (ftr/smoke); Ekely (ftr); EmiSta (br); kramer-1 (fbr/label); Ivenks (bc); mayakova (cb); ranplett (ftl); topshotUK (bl); Westlight (fcrb/corks) (cr/bottles); YawningDog (cl/ brown bottles); Alfredo dagli Orti (fr). **184 Corbis**: Gianni dagli Orti (tl). **Getty Images**: DEA / M Seemuller (bc). **184-185 The Bridgeman Art Library:** Private Collection (b). **185 The Bridgeman Art Library**: Private Collection / Johnny Van Haeften Ltd, London (tl). **Corbis**: National Nuclear Security Administration / Science Faction (tr); Stapleton Collection (br)

**Jacket images**: *Front*: **Corbis**: Randy M Ury (butterflies); **Getty Images**: Renaud Visage (wasp); **iStockphoto.com**: ODV (dynamite)

All other images © Dorling Kindersley
For further information see: www.dkimages.com